SUBVERSIVE SEAMSTER

TRANSFORM *thrift store* THREADS INTO STREET COUTURE

MELISSA ALVARADO ✳ HOPE MENG ✳ MELISSA RANNELS

[PHOTOGRAPHS BY MATTHEW CARDEN]

The Taunton Press

The Taunton Press

The Taunton Press, Inc., 63 South Main Street,
PO Box 5506, Newtown, CT 06470-5506
e-mail: tp@taunton.com

Editor: Katie Benoit
Cover & Interior design: Chika Azuma
Illustrator: Christine Erikson
Photographer: Matthew Carden

Library of Congress Cataloging-in-Publication Data
Alvarado, Melissa.
  Subversive seamster : transform thrift store threads into street couture / Melissa Alvarado,
Hope Meng, Melissa Rannels ; photographer Matthew Carden.
     p. cm.
  ISBN-13: 978-1-56158-925-8
  ISBN-10: 1-56158-925-X
 1. Clothing and dress–Alteration. 2. Clothing and dress–Remaking. I. Meng, Hope. II. Rannels, Melissa. III. Title.

TT550.A59 2007
646'.34–dc22

                              2006100608

Printed in Singapore
10 9 8 7 6 5 4 3 2 1

Dedication

Dedicated to Jeremy, Alex and Jacob—the hot and rocking Boys who always believe in our crazy shenanigans. Your unconditional love and encouragement has made all the difference.

Acknowledgments

Many exuberant thanks to everyone at The Taunton Press—Katie and Pam, the lovely sales/marketing/publicity/art folks, and Jim Childs for believing in us (again!). We are honored to work with such a wonderful group of people!

Thank you to Matt Carden for being a pleasure (as always) and snapping such lovely photos (as always). Kudos to Michael Ferris Gibson's house, Hope's Back Yard, and all the thrift shops for providing rockin' backdrops for our hot friends. Many hugs and air kisses to the foxy folks that rocked it subversive style: the Malek Sisters (Erika & Amber), the Ato Sisters (Jato & Gladys), and all the other scalding hot sisters—Jayne, Chri, Roxy, Fati, Lucid, and Hannah. Thank you to Edo Salon for your gorgeous hair styles and Carolyn Forlee for being the makeup queen! Thanks to Alissa at Mittenmaker and all the other crafty kids out there that inspire us to think outside the ready-to-wear thrift box!

As always, a special thanks to our peeps at Stitch Lounge. You provide the inspiration (and perspiration) that keeps our crafty community alive!

Contents

··· Introduction ···

You may wonder, what's the big deal with this "thrifting" thing? Isn't it a bunch of old unwanted stuff that is out of style? Not true! Sure, lots of thrift shops have outdated satin bridesmaid's frocks, old tennis racket covers, and boring bathrobes that others have carelessly tossed aside. What they don't know is that these items have the potential to be halter tops, checkbook covers, and faux feather boas with a little help from your sewing machine. *Subversive Seamster* is your secret roadmap to the jewels of thrifting and the ins and outs of refashioning. This book holds our shortcuts, tips, and secrets to the wide world of inexpensive, individualized fashion.

Subversive Seamster is all about inspiration and transformation. It's about refashioning unwanted and tired clothes and giving them a whole new life in the *front* of your closet. While any clothing can be refashioned, thrift stores are a simple (and cheap) source for all sorts of pre-refashioned treasures! All too often your fellow thrift store shoppers look for ready-to-wear items and overlook the seemingly "hideous" sweater, not picturing what glorious mittens it would make. They may toss aside that leather vest, not knowing what a fabulous pair of earrings lie inside. Silly them! Fortunately, you are wiser and won't make such a rookie mistake.

Thrift stores are not like typical clothing stores—every garment is different from the next. For any given piece, there usually is only one available, and in one size. We subversive seamsters really value this part of the thrifting experience. Shopping is that much more exciting when you discover a unique garment that truly inspires you.

We organized the chapters in this book by types of clothing, just as thrift stores are generally organized. Find a top you love at the thrift store? Discover its potential in the hot tops chapter of *Subversive Seamster!* Find a cool pattern on a pair of old man pants? Turn that fun pattern into a hot new outfit from the pants chapter. Start with an item that inspires you and go from there! Tweak our ideas, and turn them into your own. Cheap thrift store finds give you license to cut without looking back!

Don't forget to look deeper. Look beyond the old sports jersey and see its potential. What's its future? Perhaps it will become a skirt? Or maybe a change purse? Perhaps that grandma nightgown will become a grocery bag? You just never know with us subversive seamsters. We're crazy like that!

Our clothes make a statement about who we are. What better way to say, "I am an individual!" than to wear one-of-a-kind items made from other one-of-a-kind items? We derive the most fashionable satisfaction knowing that we are reusing and recycling what already exists in this material world—and looking damn good doing it!

Now c'mon, let's get our refashion on, thrift store style!

FIND THAT NEEDLE IN A HAYSTACK!

Before we delve into what you are going to do with your treasures, you have to learn how to find them first. Depending on your area, taste, and budget, you're bound to find at least one second-hand store that suits your fancy—and if you're like us, you'll find a few more than that!

When most people think thrift shops, they think of donation stores like Goodwill Industries℠ and the Salvation Army℠ (aka "Sally"), the types of businesses that take any kind of donation, sort it, and turn it around for a good cause. In addition to some of these national chains, you may find smaller shops specific to your area. To find one in your area, look in the yellow pages or do an Internet search on "thrift stores." Pricing at these shops can be all across the board, but it's usually pretty consistent within the store. Get a feel for their price point on your first visit, and keep an eye out for some good sales. Read on for our tips on sale shopping.

Be a Treasure Hunter

Besides the chains, another affordable source of thrifting treasures are yard/garage/sidewalk/estate sales. Depending on the type of area you live in, these family-oriented sales may go by different names. They mean the

same thing for you, though—good deals! Check your local newspaper classifieds or community websites (such as craigslist.org) for current sale listings, and keep your eyes peeled for signs posted in your neighborhood.

If you're into yard sales, then you'll love flea markets. Flea markets are a good way to spend a Saturday, with a plethora of secondhand sale booths all on one slab of asphalt. An icy-cold beverage and fried food on a stick will keep your energy up while shopping!

Some of the best ready-to-wear secondhand shopping outside of donation outlets is in vintage and buy-and-sell stores. These trendy shops sell handpicked clothes purchased previously by people like us. Subversive seamsters need not bother with these stores. While these shops are great for ready-to-wear items, they usually require too many ducats for the projects that lie ahead. We eschew them in favor of the Sally's and flea markets of the world. Hooray for Sally!

Second and Third and Fourth Time's a Charm

We all know that free is the best price, so if you can find someone to *give* you secondhand clothes, you're sittin' pretty. Ask friends and family members if they're itching to clean out their closets; some of the coolest things come from the depths of Grandma's wardrobe. And we all have moms who hold on to outdated fashions, right? (Thanks for being thrifty, Mom!)

Swapping unwanted clothes is a great source of free hand-me-downs. Organize a clothing swap with a few of your closest gal pals. Have each person bring a bag of clothes and a snack or drink to share. We like to sort the clothes by type (skirts, tops, dresses) and leave them untouched in piles while we sip, nosh, and socialize. Then we all take our marks, fire the starting gun, and dig like crazy through the piles. If it fits you perfectly, it goes home with you. First come, first serve! Whatever's left over can be donated to charity. These swaps can grow larger than your circle of friends. We

helped out at an event held at the local county fairground called Swap-o-Rama-Rama. Hundreds of people came through, and groups of local designers and silk screeners were on hand to help swappers customize their new treasures. Check your local craft and fashion event listings to see if something like this comes to your area.

Thrifting Tips

We're self-proclaimed thrift queens, and we're happy to share some of our trade secrets on thrifting. Keep in mind that while these tips apply to being a Subversive Seamster, they also apply to shopping for ready-to-wear clothes. (We're always a sucker for the two-for-one!) Check out these tips to get the most out of your thrifting experience.

Plan ahead

* Take a close look at the clothes you have in your closet, particularly the garments that fit you well. Get a visual idea of your size. This comes in handy if there aren't any fitting rooms at your local thrift shop. While you may not be wearing the item as is, it's good to know how much fabric the garment contains and if it's the same amount as, say, one of your favorite T-shirts.

* It's a good idea to carry a tape measure in your purse. Again, if there aren't any fitting rooms, you can get a quick idea of whether or not the garment might fit your body.

Shop like a pro

* Use a shopping cart or basket. You need free hands to sift through the racks and hold things up to your body to check the fit. Wheeled carts are ideal since handheld baskets get heavy and cumbersome. (We advocate "shop till you drop" figuratively, not literally.)

Some stores have fitting rooms, but sometimes you may not feel like putting used
clothes over your skin. It's smart
to wear a camisole and a
flowy skirt with full-coverage
undies. If there is no fitting
room, or if you're just in
a hurry, find a mirror and
hold the garments up to
your body to see if they will
stretch across your frame.
Pinch the garment along the
side seams and make sure it will
fit around your boobs, ribs, waist,
and hips. Try pants on under your skirt.

Where to begin? Start in a smaller department, like long dresses or sweaters. This
is less intimidating than diving right into knit
tops. You need to get your feet wet first.

Don't just look through the clothing racks!
The housewares section is full of secondhand
gems—cool fabrics and vintage sheets are
great material. And don't forget the accessories and sporting goods. Old leather purses,
tennis racket covers, and blankets wait pa-
tiently for you to give them new life.

Finders keepers

Once you find a garment for refashioning, consider a few things:

Are there holes or tears in the garment? Is the damaged part going
to impede your project, or can you
mend it or cut off the bad part if
necessary?

If the tear is on a seam, and you
want to use the shirt as a shirt (or
pants as pants), you can easily mend it,
so buy away!

If there's a moth hole, and you really need
that piece of the garment, think about putting
a patch or fabric appliqué over it.

If the hem on pants or shirts has unraveled
and you don't need the hem area, throw
your new treasure in your cart and keep
on shoppin'.

If you love the feel of the fabric, but hate the
color, consider dyeing the fabric the color of
your dreams! (See p. 33 for details on dyeing.)

If the garment contains a pattern or fabric
you like, you can always do something with it.

If the parts you need are damaged or torn, don't be afraid to mix and match to get the amount of fabric you need.

❋ Is it stained? Can you cut out the stain or wash it? Is the price worth it? Can you get a discount? (Never hurts to ask!)

❋ Does it smell? Can you wash out the smell? How difficult will it be to wash the fabric?

- Polyester is easy to wash (though it can hold odors).

- Silk typically needs to be dry-cleaned, which can get a little spendy, so we shy away from it.

- Cotton is easy to wash, but it's also easy to shrink, so make sure you've got more than enough fabric for your project.

❋ Note "dry-clean only" tags— these may be a deal breaker. (If it's cheap and you love it, buy it anyway, and try throwing it in the wash. If you ruin it, oh well!)

❋ Be sure to check for materials that you are comfortable wearing. Many vintage clothes are made with heavy polyester, which is not very breathable and can be uncomfortable to wear. Similarly, some people are allergic to wool and other fibers. Be sure to choose a material that is right for you.

❋ Will you have to iron it after you wash it? (We are sometimes too excited about our clothes to spend time ironing, so we frown upon required ironing.)

- If it's cotton, satin, or rayon, you will most likely have to iron it.

- If it's polyester, you will be wrinkle-free from the get-go!

Eagle eyes

Keep an eye out for anything unique and unusual. Secondhand stores can be a treasure trove of off-the-wall patterns, fabrics, and colors. Embrace those colors and patterns and admire their evolution through the decades!

❋ Polyester is easy to work with since it is such a pliable material, but it's not always so breathable.

* Cotton may be tricky depending on how worn or thin it is, but in general it is manageable.

* Satin and rayon (oh, the '80s!) can be tough since they're so slippery, but go ahead if you are up for the challenge!

* Lycra® can be challenging to work with, but its stretch is forgiving, and we love that!

* Although fabric may be the first thing that catches your attention, pay attention to other details when shopping.

  • Take a minute to search out the form: We're talking about waistbands, shoulders, bodices, cuffs, A-lines, empire waists, and so on. You can always remove the undesired portions of a garment, but if it's got a unique form, you should definitely take advantage of it.

  • Find garments that have more than one piece—like a jacket and dress, or pants and a vest—two for the price of one!

• A slow and careful eye will also catch details like buttons, zippers, collars, and belts—things that can be removed from their original garment for use on something else.

Know when to hold 'em, know when to fold 'em

Always try to make a deal with the seller. Keep an eye out for motivated sellers, especially at yard sales and flea markets. Donation store employees generally have less flexibility to make deals.

* Try asking for a deal if you're buying a lot, especially from a yard sale or an independent thrift store.

* No matter where you are, if you love it and it has a huge hole or stain, it never hurts to ask for a break.

* Many stores have revolving sales—ask about them, or look for posted ads and signs in windows.

❋ Some stores have different-colored price tags and offer Orange Mondays or Blue Sundays, when discounts are given on items with those colored tags.

❋ Keep your ears open! If you're in a store long enough, you may hear an announcement over the loudspeaker like, "Hey everybody, it's 2 o'clock and it's jacket hour! All jackets are $2 for the next 60 minutes." Talk about being in the right place at the right time!

Back at the ranch

When you're done shopping, it's time to get things clean.

❋ Wash your hands after you leave the store.

❋ Always wash everything you buy, even if it still has its original tags. It's the character of the garment, not that of the previous owner, that you're interested in. It's smart to wash all pieces so they can start their new life on a clean foot.

Most importantly, don't limit yourself to clothes that fit you! As you'll see in *Subversive Seamster*, grab anything that catches your eye. It may be a too-big shirt with an interesting pattern, or out-of-style pants made of a cool fabric. Train your eye to see potential!

With a little prepping, some basic fabric knowledge, and an eagle eye, thrift shops are a vast land of possibilities and shopping goodness.

• • • A Quick History Tip • • •

During World War II, war production took up many of the natural resources (especially fibers), so ration coupons were issued for items that included clothing. But even during war times, people still wanted to look fashionable, and two ways to get around rationing (besides the black market) included buying secondhand clothes and repairing or remaking (i.e., refashioning) old clothes. The government offered encouragement by issuing booklets on how to refashion your old garments!

SEWING 201

It's time to kick your sewing skills up a notch. Mending a hole and sewing on a button are great foundation techniques, but this chapter will help you get an even better fit out of your fashion and increase the flair factor of your refashioning skills. We'll go over the techniques that you need for the projects in later chapters, so you'll be well equipped to create your own designs!

Corner Your Pivoting Skills!

We all know that pillows, curtains, and place-mats can have sharp corners, but so can garments. To make your corners nice and square, finish your seam with the needle *in* the fabric at the corner. Lift up the presser foot, and pivot the fabric around the needle to set up your next line of stitches. Lower the presser foot and continue sewing.

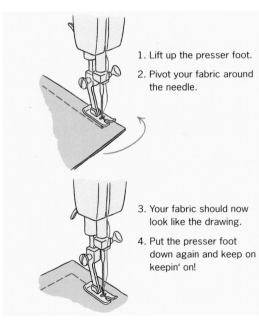

1. Lift up the presser foot.
2. Pivot your fabric around the needle.

3. Your fabric should now look like the drawing.
4. Put the presser foot down again and keep on keepin' on!

Top This Decorative Stitching Technique

Topstitching is an easy, cheap way to add your own unique touch to existing garments. It may not surprise you, but topstitching is stitching on top of your material (the party side or "good side") rather than on the business side (or "bad side"). Before you sew the pieces of a garment together, you can zip your machine over the fabric to make decorative patterns. Try using several different colors of thread or contrasting pattern shapes for an even funkier look.

Flower Power

Fabric flowers are an easy way to liven up any boring garment. Use the leftover material from your project to make a flower that matches your piece, or mix and match fabrics for some seriously fun style.

STEP 1: SEW A TUBE

To make a fabric flower out of leftover material, take a long strip of fabric and sew the ends together to make a circle.

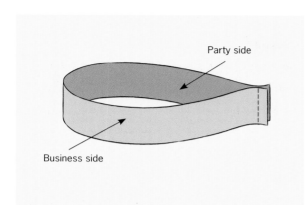

Party side

Business side

STEP 2: GATHER IT UP

Then use a hand needle and thread to make a loose stitch around the bottom of this tube.

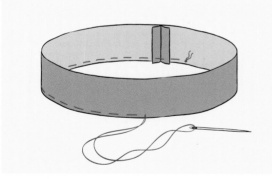

When you pull the thread taut, *voilà*! It's a flower!

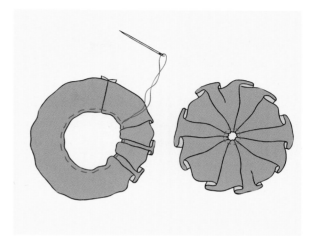

Everyone Loves Patches

Patch pockets are really easy to make and are not only a practical element for any garment or accessory, but also a good opportunity to add some unexpected pizzazz to an otherwise boring piece.

STEP 1: MEASURE AND CUT

Start by getting some leftover fabric from another project. Determine how large you want your patch pocket to be and add 1 inch to the width and the height of the pocket for seam allowances. If you want a 5-inch by 7-inch pocket, cut a 6-inch by 8-inch square of fabric.

STEP 2: FINISH THE EDGES

Fold each edge over ½ inch and iron the folds down. Using a straight stitch with a medium stitch length, sew the folds down. Turn the corners as you go.

STEP 3: TOPSTITCH IT ON

Pin your pocket in place and topstitch on three sides, leaving the top open so you can put your goods in it later.

make it your way

Experiment with shapes other than squares and rectangles. Circles and other shapes are decorative, practical, and totally unexpected!

Use contrasting fabric or thread for your patch pocket to add even more pizzazz to your project!

Lettuce Show You a Great Finishing Technique!

Lettuce edging is a flirty, feminine way to finish off your rough edges. And best of all, it's super easy to do.

STEP 1: SET YOUR MACHINE

Start by setting your sewing machine to a zig-zag stitch with a wide stitch width and short to medium stitch length. Position your fabric underneath the presser foot so that when the machine is making its zigzag, the needle doesn't hit any

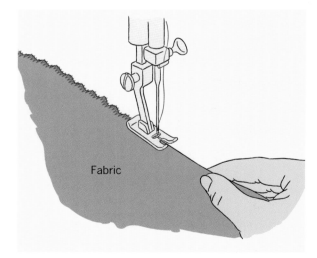

Fabric

fabric on one side. (Use your machine's hand wheel to see where the needle will come down, and position your fabric accordingly.)

STEP 2: ZIGZAG THE EDGE

Lettuce edging is a lot like ruching in that you pull on the fabric before it goes underneath the presser foot. (We're going to cover ruching next.) Start sewing your zigzag stitch so that the zigzag crosses over the cut edge of the fabric, pulling the fabric toward you before it goes underneath the presser foot.

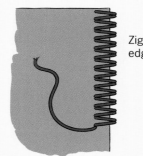

Zigzag hangs over edge of fabric

STEP 3: ADMIRE YOUR WORK

Ta-daa! You've made a fun, frilly edge that also binds the cut edge of your fabric!

Ruche Me Up, Ruche Me Down

Ruching uses elastic to gather extra fabric while still allowing for some stretch. We use ruching to make a baggy fit more flattering.

STEP 1: MEASURE

First, decide what part of the garment you want to ruche. For example, do you want to ruche underneath your bustline, gathering the fabric and enhancing your Girls? (Yes, you do!) Or maybe you want to ruche around the wrist hems of your long-sleeved tee for a peasant effect. Either way, you'll need to get a measurement of the area you want to ruche. If you want to gather the fabric underneath your bust, measure the circumference of your rib cage below The Girls. If you want to ruche the hem of your long-sleeved shirt, measure around your wrist.

STEP 2: CUT AND STITCH

Cut a piece of elastic to the length of the measurement you just took. Turn your garment inside out and chalk a line where you want the ruching. Sew one end of the elastic to the beginning of this line using a zigzag stitch with a wide stitch width and medium stitch length.

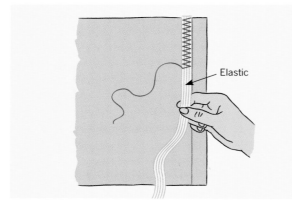

Continue sewing the elastic to your garment along your chalkline, pulling gently on the elastic before it goes underneath the presser foot. This is a little tricky, but you can do it—just go slowly.

STEP 3: TRIM AND FINISH

You will probably have extra elastic when you get to the end of your chalkline, so just cut it off after you backtack the seam. You do not want all this work to come undone! Good job, lady! You're a ruching queen!

Casing the Joint

What's a casing, you ask? Picture your most comfy pajama bottoms. The tube that the drawstring or the elastic band sits inside is called a casing. Casings are easy to make and quite helpful when putting together a drawstring pouch.

STEP 1: CHECK YOUR BANDWIDTH

The width of your casing depends on the width of your drawstring or elastic. You want to allow for a little wiggle room but not too much, especially if you're using elastic. (If you make your casing much wider than your elastic, the elastic can twist, which is annoying and makes your waistband lumpy. This isn't as much of an issue with a drawstring, but it can happen to ribbon as well, so it's best to play it safe.)

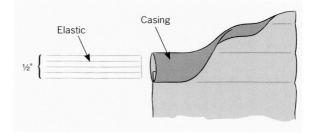

STEP 2: KNOW WHEN TO FOLD 'EM

If your casing is meant to house an elastic
waistband, fold the elastic in half to make a
circle and zigzag the cut edges together using
a wide stitch width and a medium stitch length.
You should have a giant rubber band at this
point. Place the elastic so it is encircling the
waist portion of the pants, fold over the edge
of the fabric (business side to business side),
and pin it into place. Make sure the amount
you fold over is the width of your casing plus
½ inch for seam allowance.

If your casing is for a drawstring pouch, you will need to make two buttonholes for the ends of the ribbon. You will want to place the buttonholes a little more than ½ inch (seam allowance) below the cut edge of the fabric plus the width of the ribbon. In other words, if you are using 1-inch-wide ribbon, your buttonholes will start a little more than 1½ inches below the cut edge of the fabric.

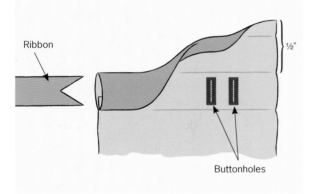

Ribbon

½"

Buttonholes

With the item or garment business-side out, place one end of the ribbon through one of the buttonholes and string the ribbon around the item, placing the other end through the other buttonhole. (See top illustration at right)

Once the drawstring is in place, fold over the edge of the fabric (business side to business side) and pin it into place. Make sure the amount you fold over is the width of your drawstring plus ½ inch for seam allowance.

STEP 3: I REST MY CASE

Sew your casing using a straight stitch for woven fabrics or a zigzag stitch for knits, being careful not to stitch over the elastic or ribbon. Remember that your stitches will show on the

Stitch here.

party side of your garment, so use a thread color that is appropriate and sew your stitches as straight as you can.

Get All Ruffled Up

Adding ruffles is a simple way to add a feminine touch to shirtsleeves or to add volume to the plain silhouette of a skirt. To start, you'll need a strip of fabric or some trim, like ribbon or lace. Remember that whatever you decide to use, you'll lose a little of its height to seam allowance, so plan accordingly.

STEP 1: TACK IT IN PLACE

To commence ruffling, start by tacking one edge of the strip to the garment you're working on, wherever you want your ruffle to begin. Use a

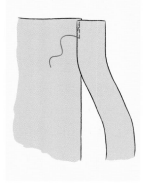

¼-inch seam allowance for the strip and the edge of the garment.

Tack the strip in place by using a straight stitch with a medium stitch length. Sew for about 1 inch and backtack.

If you want a finished look, tack the party side of the strip to the business side of the garment. This way your stitches and rough edges will hide inside the finished garment.

If you prefer a rougher, more deconstructed look, tack the business side of the strip to the party side of the garment, so the rough edge of the strip is on the outside of the garment. (This works really well with denim because it frays in the wash.)

If you're using your ruffle to add decoration, and not attaching it to an edge of the garment (like the ruffles on the front of a tuxedo shirt), tack the ruffle to the garment so that the business side of the strip faces the party side of the garment, but stitch the strip down the middle of the ruffle instead of along the edge. For a clean, non-fraying edge, you can hem the edges of the strip before sewing them on.

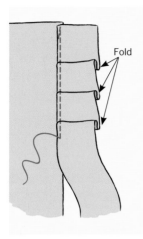

Fold

STEP 2: RUFFLES HAVE RIDGES

Sew along for about an inch. Now make a fold in the same direction as your stitching and hold it in place with your fingers. Sew over the fold and in a straight line for another inch or so (see the illustration above). Keep making this folding pattern as you sew on your strip and watch your ruffle come to life.

Take It in a Notch

Whether the waist is too big, your Girls are hidden in too much fabric, or your small hips are swimming in pants designed for a most curvaceous figure, learning to take in your garments is the key to getting the perfect fit. Using Ms. Double Trouble, your duct tape body double, makes this process much easier (see p. 34). If you don't have a Ms. Trouble in your life, you can still use this technique on your own body—it will just take a little longer.

STEP 1: PARTY ON THE INSIDE

Make sure you turn the garment business-side out before you slip it onto Ms. Trouble or yourself. You'll be placing pins in the garment so that the lines you create with the pins are the lines that fit your body. Try to take in along the existing seams of the garment when possible, like the side seams of a skirt or shirt.

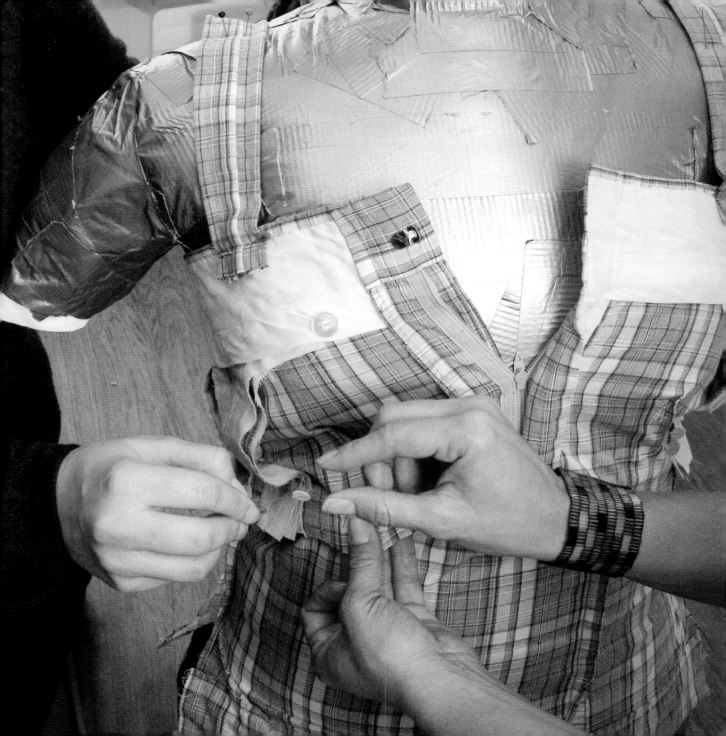

STEP 2: HUGGING THOSE CURVES

Once your garment is all pinned, take it off your body or Ms. Trouble and over to the sewing machine. Using a medium straight stitch (or a small zigzag stitch if you're taking in a knit), sew along the curved lines of your pins, removing them as you go along.

At the beginnings and ends of these seams, try to get the stitches to match the existing edge of the fabric—that way, you won't get a pleat or a bubble in your garment. You don't have to be exact, but try to follow the curve of the existing edge so the garment will fall on your figure in the most flattering way possible.

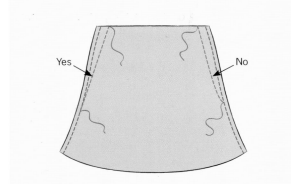

Darts, Anyone?

If you need to take in a part of your garment where there are no seams—like the fabric under your bust, in the curve of your lower back, or just below a waistband on the back side of pants, you'll be adding darts. Darting is what takes a boxy, square top and transforms it into a fitted, sexy, lady-rific top. Adding a dart is like taking in a garment in a more specialized way.

STEP 1: DARING TO DART

With the garment business-side out, and on your own body or Ms. Trouble's, pinch the fabric that you want removed, and pin a curved line in that space. When darting a top, it is most common to run two darts vertically down the front and/or back, making sure the darts are evenly spaced from the center of the shirt.

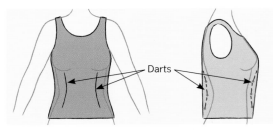

STEP 2: BULL'S-EYE

Using a short straight stitch (or a short, narrow zigzag stitch for knits), sew along the curved lines of your pins, remembering to pull them out as you go.

At the beginning and end of your stitch line, try to get the stitches to ease off at the appropriate angle, rather than make an abrupt stop. If your stitches come in perpendicular to the edge of the fabric, you'll create a pleat, or a bubbled spot in the garment.

We Like Buttonholes and We Cannot Lie

As ladies who *love* buttons, we also love buttonholes! But buttonholes aren't just for buttons; they are also a great way to bind off small holes in your garment that you might use for threading ribbon (they go very well with casings). Since this can be a tricky process the first couple of times you do it, be sure to practice on a scrap of fabric before working on your garment. Then you can test the buttonhole with your buttons to make sure it's a good fit!

STEP 1: SIZING UP THE SITUATION

Before you get started, figure out how long you want your buttonhole to be. You usually want the buttonhole to be just a wee bit taller than the button it will house and not much more, otherwise your buttons may wander out of their homes. A standard buttonhole height can vary depending on the case, but generally it should be no taller than 125 percent of the button height. Measure well and mark off the desired length with some chalk or a couple of pins.

Most modern sewing machines come with a buttonhole setting on the stitch pattern selector. It probably looks something like this:

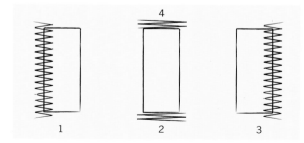

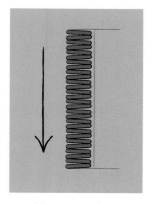

If you see this on your machine, set your stitch pattern selector to make the stitch that reads "1."

If you don't have a buttonhole selection on your machine, never fear! Just set your machine to make a zigzag stitch with a medium stitch width and a short stitch length. Stitch the length of your desired buttonhole.

STEP 2:
TOP IT OFF

For you lucky ladies who have the machines with the buttonhole pattern, now is the time to turn your stitch pattern selector to make the stitch that reads "2." For the rest of us, we're going to set our machine to make a zigzag stitch with the widest stitch width and a zero stitch length. That's right—zero! Press the foot pedal so that the machine sews about three to four zigzag stitches in place. Make sure your needle stops on the right side of the zigzag.

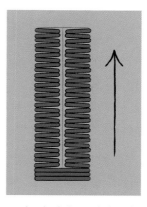

STEP 3:
COMING DOWN
THE HOME
STRETCH

OK, lucky ladies, turn your stitch pattern selector to stitch "3," and everyone else, turn your stitch width and stitch length back to the same settings that you had in step 1. Lucky ladies, sew the other side of the buttonhole to match the length from step 1. Everyone else, depress the reverse button and do the same.

STEP 4: MAKING THE CONNECTION

OK, now let's close this baby up! Lucky ladies, flip your stitch pattern selector over to—you guessed it— to stitch "4" or "2" (some machines use the same selection for this step) and everyone else gets to set the stitch width back to the widest width and the stitch length back to zero. Sew about three to four zigzag stitches in place, connecting the stitch you made in step 1 to the stitch you made in step 3.

STEP 5: SNIP IT

We're so close! Now use a small, sharp pair of scissors or your trusty seam ripper to cut a hole where the button will slip through. Congratulations! You just made a buttonhole!

It's Hard Out There for a Pin Tuck

A pin tuck is a narrow fold of fabric sewn together that gives a decorative raised look on a garment, but it also serves as a stylish way to take in a little material.

STEP 1: SIZE IT UP

Since each pin tuck is like a little ridge, it takes up twice the amount of fabric as its height. So, a ¼-inch pin tuck will take in about ½ inch of fabric. Generally, we keep our pin tucks around ¼ inch. If you want your garment to be 1 inch smaller, it will have two pin tucks, each taking up ½ inch of fabric and standing ¼ inch tall. (1 inch ÷ ½ inch of fabric = 2 pin tucks, each ¼ inch tall) You can pinch the fabric a little to see how a pin tuck will look. You can do several columns of pin tucks to take in several inches of fabric.

STEP 2: GET DECISIVE

Decide how many pin tucks you want on your garment and where to put them. With your material party-side out, fold the fabric where you want the ridge of the pin tuck to be. If you like, you can iron down that ridge. It makes things easy under the sewing machine, but it's not necessary.

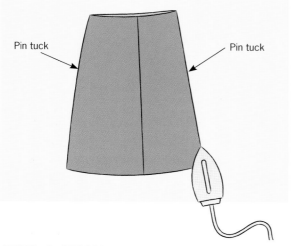

STEP 3: TUCK

Starting at one end, stitch a line ¼ inch in from the ridge (using the outer edge of your presser foot as a guide). Sew all the way down the edge

of your fabric. You should backtack the beginning and end of a pin tuck.

You can repeat this step on either side of the first tuck to make as many tucks as you'd like.

Cutting Tips

We've spent a lot of time deconstructing cloth-ing, so we've got some cutting tips for you! Follow these tips, and spend more time rockin' your new clothes than your seam ripper.

Edgy Edges

Most manufactured clothing is sewn with a serger, a machine that wraps thread around the edge of a garment so that the seam looks like this:

Serged edges can be a pain to undo with a seam ripper. If you are just using the back piece of a shirt, for instance, cut just to the far side of the seam line so that the serged edge stays with the piece you want to use. That way, you have a nice, finished edge on the piece you just cut off!

Use this technique when you replace sleeves on a shirt (leave the serged edge on the shirt, not the sleeves), when cutting the bodice off a dress (leave the serged edge on the bod-ice), and so on.

Garment Maximus

When cutting a piece out of an existing garment, maximize what you've got. Instead of cutting out

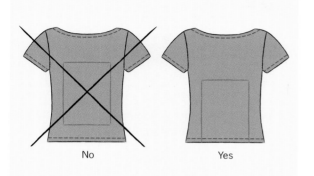

No   Yes

of the middle of the garment, cut the piece out so that you can use the finished edges.

Instead of four raw edges, you've already got one finished side!

Dyeing for Some Color

Before you dye clothing, read the instructions on the back of your dye bottle. Every brand is a little different, and you don't want to make a mistake with dye. You usually have the choice of dyeing in your washing machine or sink. Dyeing in the washing machine is nice, but we hate

the extensive cleanup process afterward. We like to play it safe by dyeing our fabric in a large plastic bin in the bathtub. Again, consult the instructions on the back of the dye bottle for the specifics.

When dyeing in a plastic bin, be sure to get the item of clothing completely wet before putting it in the dye. This helps the fabric take up the color evenly. You'll want to stir the whole concoction constantly to make sure you are getting nice, even coverage on your fabric. There is nothing worse than spending a bunch of time dyeing only to find streaks of lighter color across the garment because the fabric bunched in the bin. So stir your brew!

Once your garment has been in the dye long enough, rinse it in water (if the instructions say to do so) until the water runs clear. You might want to do this in a stainless steel sink, as the dye can turn your bathtub all kinds of psychedelic colors if you're not careful! Throw the garment in the washing machine and run a normal cycle with warm water and detergent.

Ms. Double Trouble: The Duct Tape Dress Form

By now you should have learned that hemming and altering clothes while they're on your body can pose a bit of a challenge. You lift your arm to adjust a strap, the rest of the shirt pulls up over your tummy, and you're reduced to blindly placing pins. Sewing with a buddy solves this problem and is always more fun, but sometimes buddies aren't around for late-night sewing benders when you really need someone to pin the shoulder of your shirt. Enter Double Trouble, the dress form—Ms. Trouble, to you.

A dress form is a full-scale duplicate of your body (only probably not as cute) from mid-neck to below the derriere, usually with short sleeves (imagine a minidress with a turtleneck collar and short sleeves). Dress forms are pinnable and can be posed on a stand to adjust their height. There are all sorts of dress forms out there— some are covered in fabric and are size-adjustable with a few screws, while others are high-tech custom-made body scans. Most are on the expensive side and never quite seem to mirror your exact figure.

The solution is the inexpensive DIY duct tape dress form Ms. Trouble. Ms. Trouble will come to life as one of your (trusted) friends wraps you like a mummy in plastic wrap and silver duct

tape. The reason we recommend duct tape is because of its super stick-ability, low cost, and width. And, really, let's face it, who doesn't love duct tape? You can also use paper tape for this project (the kind you use to seal boxes when you're shipping a care package). Paper tape is good because it doesn't get as gummy as duct tape, and it spares the blades of your scissors when you're cutting yourself out of the dress form.

Ms. Trouble should mirror your fabulous curve distribution, the slope of your shoulders, your bootyliciousness, and everything in between. Soon you and Ms. Trouble will be pinning straps, darting shirts, and taking in waistbands like it was nothing.

WHAT YOU'LL NEED

* a large, longish T-shirt you are willing to sacrifice
* two rolls of duct tape (you may need a third roll if you are size extra-large or larger or if you like to get crazy with the amount of taping)
* plastic wrap
* batting (like pillow stuffing)
* a wrapping buddy
* scissors (not your fabric scissors, but a sharp pair that you do not mind getting a little gunked up—any sturdy kind will do)

TIME TO COMPLETE

2 to 2½ hours per person

STEP 1: PREP

Use the ladies' room. It may sound obvious, but make sure to use the restroom before starting this project, as it is quite difficult to maneuver in a duct tape getup, and you'll be wrapped up for well over an hour.

Put a large T-shirt on over your normal underthings. (It should be long enough to cover your tush. Attach a piece of plastic wrap (with duct tape, of course!) to make your tee into a turtleneck. Remember, you don't want the tape to adhere to your skin, so if you don't want that exposed skin to be part of Ms. Trouble, cover it with plastic wrap. Then tape plastic wrap to the bottom of the T-shirt to create a midthigh-length skirt. Again, cover *all* skin, pants, and undergarments with plastic wrap before taping them up.

STEP 2: WRAP

Have your friend wrap you horizontally, starting midthigh and heading up. She should wrap you snugly, as the duct tape is supposed to be an approximation of your undressed figure. Be careful to overlap the edges of the duct tape by a smidge so everything stays together. Make sure you start taping over the plastic wrap, and if your plastic "skirt" is a bit longer than where you start taping, you can trim it off when you finish up.

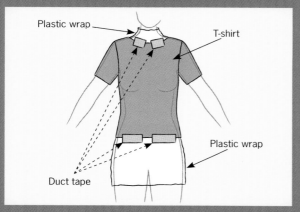

Plastic wrap

T-shirt

Plastic wrap

Duct tape

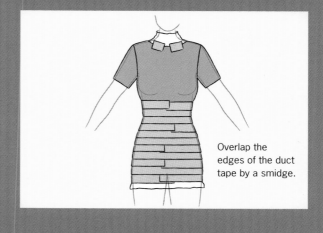

Overlap the edges of the duct tape by a smidge.

Keep wrapping around until you get right underneath your bust. Use short strips of tape to create a flower-shaped pattern across your boob, with each piece of tape being a petal. This will help make sure you accurately reflect your chest size. Then make a crisscross X in the middle of your chest, going from shoulder to waist to add to the contours of your décolletage.

After the chest contouring is done, make shoulder straps of duct tape. Starting from where you left off on your back, tape over your shoulder to the top of your boob flower. Make these "straps" across your entire back and

shoulders. If there is a tricky angle, it's OK to improvise and stick some tape to make sure the T-shirt is covered. Not all the straps need to go all the way over your shoulder; just make sure the entire upper torso part of the tee is covered with duct tape. We now move on to the sleeves and neck.

Place strips of tape from the top of your shoulder (where a bra strap might sit) and down your arm to form short sleeves. We find it easier to tape in vertical stripes for the sleeves first, as it creates a faux boning and prevents your potentially exuberant friend from making a too-tight blood pressure cuff on your arm. Now wrap horizontally around the short sleeve you created, taping to the middle of your biceps or wherever your T-shirt ends. The angle of the arms is up to you. We recommend they be at least a 45-degree angle out from your side to make sure you can fit garments underneath.

Then, create the turtleneck portion of Ms. Trouble by taping around the neck. Continue until you are a couple of inches up the neck. Watch out for stray neck hairs!

Using long strips of tape, have your friend
do a final wrap on your bottom half, but this
time, instead of wrapping around, tape vertical

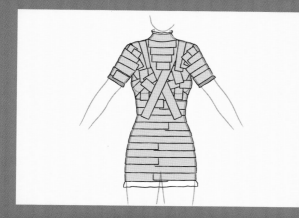

strips up and down. Make sure the strips are
even and smooth, as they will be your final layer.
We're almost done, don't worry!

STEP 3: MARK

When everything's a wrap (bad pun intended),
have your buddy mark your belly button with per-
manent marker, which will give you a good visual
indication of where the waistband of a skirt will
sit on your body when Ms. Trouble is modeling
it for you. It will also provide a height indicator if

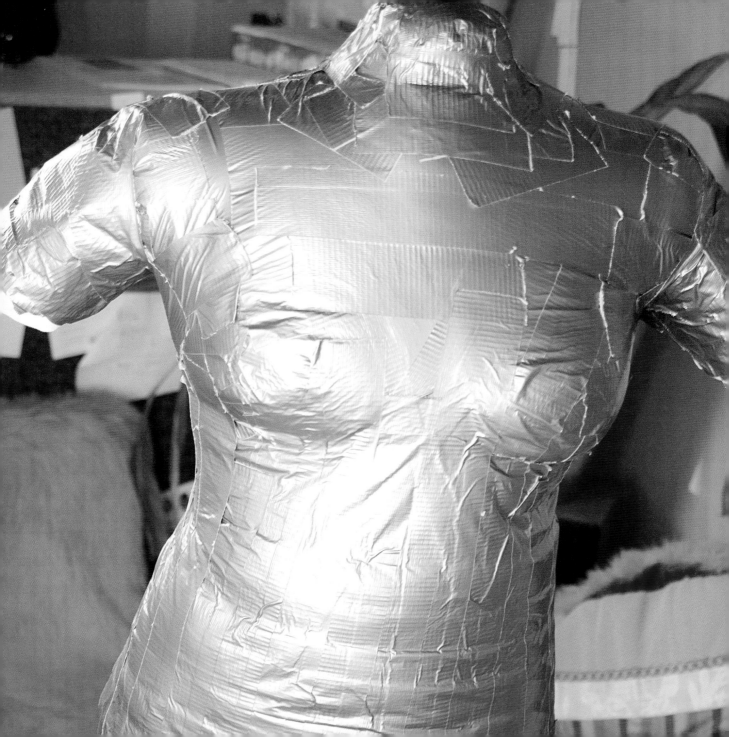

you want to put Ms. Trouble on a stand. (More on that in a minute.) If there is any part of you that you'd like to remember when designing clothes (tattoos, freckles, parts you'd rather not be visible or parts you *really* want visible), now is the time to mark 'em!

STEP 4: CUT

Have your friend cut very, very carefully up the center of your back. Make sure she doesn't snip your bra or panties (or skin for that matter!), so no laughing. Remove yourself from Ms. Trouble, put your normal clothes back on again, and use the ladies' room, finally!

Now, check out Ms. Trouble! She looks good! Close up the seam with, yes, more duct tape. Double-check her measurements with a measuring tape. Compare bust, waist, and hips to your own. (It's OK if you are a little off, but it should be relatively close.)

Stuff Ms. Trouble with batting until she is squeezable and pinnable, but not easily com-pressed. Check the measurements one more time and adjust the amount of stuffing as needed. Once you are satisfied with the shape, close off the arm and neck holes with more duct tape, by taping across the opening in a flower petal manner (like the way you covered your boobs earlier). We like to cover the back cut with one long vertical piece down the length of the dress form and several horizontal "stitches" of tape going across. You have the option of using a standing lamp base (we all have an old halogen stand lying around) or microphone stand to hold her up. Stick the pole in before closing up the bottom, and measure the height from your belly button to the floor, then use the same height for Ms. Trouble's marked belly button. Secure the stand with, you guessed it, more duct tape, and, *voilà*, you have a full-size carbon copy of you, just waiting to help you sew! Now play nice, and help your friend make her own Ms. Trouble. Let's get crackin'!

HOT TOPS

Tops are a great place to start your thrifting adventure! They're cheap and plentiful—available in every size, shape, color, and material under the vintage rainbow. Look for cool patterns and forgotten polyester shirts. Remember, size doesn't always matter! Big tops mean more material to work with, and small tops can be put to use as pillow covers or coin purses. Leather vests provide a reasonably priced piece of leather, which you can turn into unreasonably cute earrings. And don't forget the jacket section! The wool coat of yesteryear may become today's adorable wool skirt! Now let's get you on top of your thrifting game!

Sham on You

We all have some drab pillows sitting around that are just not our style or are slightly outdated and could use a little makeover. Now's the time to hone your mad thrifting skills and make some new pillow shams for those bad boys! Please note that while we are generally in favor of thrifting items, we don't recommend you get your pillow forms that way, as they may be lumpy and mis-shapen and are expensive to clean. Splurge (and by *splurge*, we mean "spend $10") on new forms from a fabric store, use your old pillows as forms, or snag some from a trusted source—like Mom or a friend who is moving. We do recommend, however, that you hit the thrift stores for the button-down shirts that you'll use to make the covers. Make sure your shirt has buttons all the way up the front (or at least the length of the pillow). Grab one in a funky print to match your funky style! You might also want to consider matching your couch or bed, but that's your choice. Remember that these are loud, funky pillows with buttons, so they should be smaller accent pieces, like throw pillows.

WHAT YOU'LL NEED
- Hawaiian shirt (or other printed button-down shirt)
- pillow (that needs covering)

TECHNIQUES YOU'LL USE
- turning corners

TIME TO COMPLETE
45 minutes

STEP 1: SIZE YOUR PILLOW

In order to know how much fabric you'll need for the front and back of your sham, measure your pillow. Take the width and add 1 inch for a seam allowance. Do the same for the height. We are covering a 16-inch by 16-inch pillow, so we will need two 17-inch by 17-inch squares of fabric.

Lay your shirt out flat and make sure you've got enough fabric to cover your pillow. If you don't have enough yardage, never fear! Just pick a larger shirt or a smaller pillow. Next, determine where the button line should sit on your pillow. The pillow form will be inserted through the button opening, so make sure it is not too far off to one side. We dig diagonals (buttons centered

straight down the middle are for other people!), so our button line will go from corner to corner on our pillow.

STEP 2: GET TO CUTTIN'

Trace your width and length measurements onto the shirt and cut through both layers to get identically sized front and back pieces. (If there's a part of the pattern you want to capture on the back side of the pillow that is not directly in line with the front, you can cut the front separately from the back.)

STEP 3: SEWING 'ROUND AND 'ROUND

Facing party side to party side, use a straight

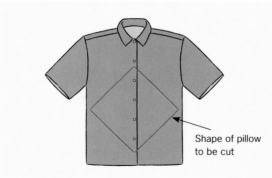

Shape of pillow
to be cut

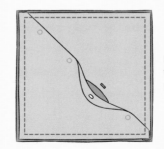

Reach under
the flap and
unbutton

stitch with a medium stitch length to sew around the entire square (or rectangle), leaving a ½-inch seam allowance. After you have expertly pivoted all the corners, unbutton the pillowcase so you can turn it party-side out.

STEP 4: SHARPEN YOUR CORNERS

Once the pillowcase is ready, use a pointed but relatively blunt object (like a retracted pen) to push the corners out so they are nice and sharp. Unbutton the shirt fully and insert your pillow form. Button up that snazzy new sham and mentally transport yourself to the nearest tropical island. Being ridiculously stylish has never been easier!

make it your way

You can use virtually any type of shirt or jacket with button closures (or even a zipper if you dare!) to make cute pillow shams. Sift through the thrift store racks and find the cowboy shirts, uniforms, or funky '70s shirts of your dreams!

The Vest Earrings in Town

"In fashion, either you are in or you are out." Leather vests used to be in; now they have been sent packing. But don't worry, we can use the cast-offs to our advantage. Let's make them into earrings! You heard us—earrings! Here, we make a cute but easy leaf-shaped pair for you to rock around the town in. Leather vests, you have been warned!

WHAT YOU'LL NEED

* leather vest
* awl or thick needle
* earring loops (these can be found at craft stores, bead stores, and jewelry supply locales)
* leather needle
* special sewing machine foot (optional—see step 2)
* needle-nose pliers

TECHNIQUES YOU'LL USE

* topstitching

TIME TO COMPLETE

30 minutes

STEP 1: CUT IT OUT AND LINE IT UP

Cut four 3-inch squares of leather out of your vest. Take two pieces and face the business sides together. Do the same with your other two pieces. Don't pin these pieces, as the holes will remain in the leather if you do.

STEP 2: LEATHER RIP

Sewing leather can be tricky because it will stretch underneath a normal sewing machine foot. Many people use a special Teflon® foot or a walking foot when sewing leather, but the ladies of *Subversive Seamster* aren't like most people, and we expect you're not either.

For a small project like this, you have two options. Either you can live with the stretching and even plan your design around it (notice how well the leaf shape we chose for our earrings works with the stretch of the leather), or you can minimize the stretch by using a zipper foot (usually included with most machines). Since a zipper foot has less surface area than a normal foot, it doesn't stick as much to the leather. And sewing two pieces of leather together will help

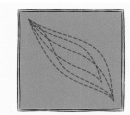

Topstitched leaves on
leather square

minimize the stretch a bit, too.

Using the method that suits you, sew a straight stitch with a long stitch length, topstitching some design onto your 3-inch squares. Remember, you can make circles, squares, or any other shape your little heart desires.

STEP 3: TRIM IT DOWN

Cut the leather pieces so approximately ⅛ inch of leather is left around your stitching. Sewing before cutting is important because it can be difficult to sew perfect stitches close to the edge.

STEP 4: PUNCH IT UP A NOTCH

Using your awl (or a thick needle), punch a hole at the top of your design. Pry open the loops on your earring hardware using some needle-nose pliers. Slip the leather pieces onto the loops, and you've got yourself some pretty hip ear décor or a great gift for a friend!

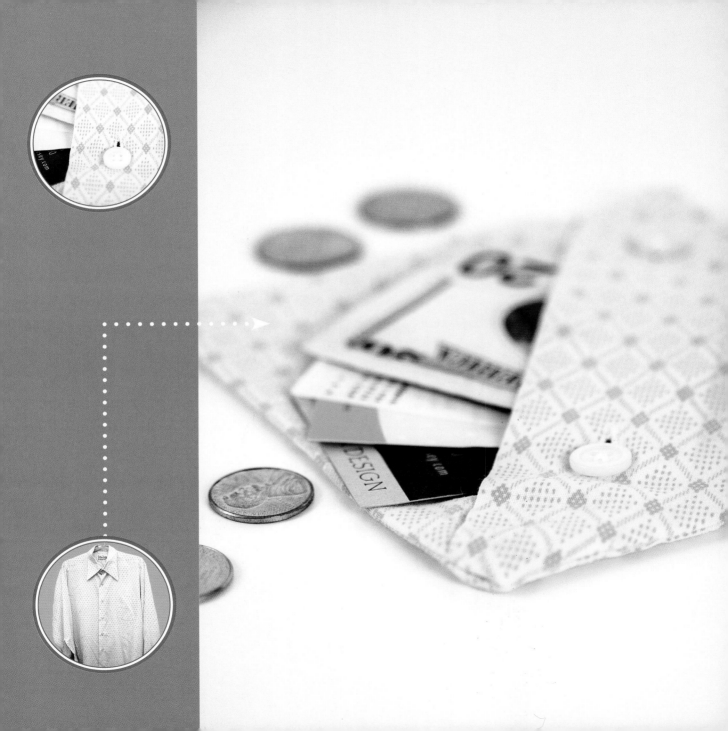

Coin a New Purse!

Tackle that pile of button-down men's shirts at your local thrift shop to make this little coin purse. Get creative—use any buttoned part of the shirt. Since you need such a small amount of fabric, two pieces approximately 6 inches by 6 inches, check in your scrap bin before cutting up a whole new shirt.

WHAT YOU'LL NEED

❋ button-down shirt

TECHNIQUES YOU'LL USE

❋ embellishing

❋ turning corners

TIME TO COMPLETE

30 minutes

STEP 1: CUT IT OUT

Choose a portion of the shirt to use for your purse. You can use the front buttons or even a button pocket, but any portion of the shirt with existing and corresponding buttonholes will do the trick. We like a diagonal look, so we cut a square shape with the opening running diagonally across it. Make sure to cut a back piece that's the same size and shape as the front piece with the buttons, but cut the back piece from a section of the shirt that does not have an opening.

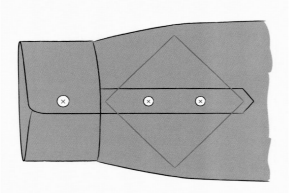

STEP 2: EMBELLISH THE BACK SIDE

Since the back panel is plain fabric, feel free to embellish it a bit. But if your shirt already has a decorative print, you might want to downplay the embellishments.

STEP 3: SEW IT CLOSED

Before you sew the purse shut, check the opening to make sure that your goods won't fall out. If you need to sew the opening up, now is the time. Sew just enough of the opening so your stuff can go in and stay in!

Now, facing the party side of the front piece to the party side of the back piece, sew around the square using a straight stitch with a medium to short stitch length. Be sure to pivot around the needle when tuning the corners (see p. 16 for more on turning corners). Trim the extra fabric off the corners, unbutton the opening, and turn the purse party-side out. Use a blunt object to push the corners out so they are sharp, then throw some change in your pouch and hold your bus fare in style.

the Repair

Warm Limbs, Cool Lady

Thrift shops always seem to have sweaters aplenty! Some are cute and some are, well, not so cute. Find one with a pattern you dig, and feel free to disregard everything else not-so-cute about it. We're gonna make mittens and arm warmers to keep you warm and lookin' hot! (We recommend you wear the mittens and arm warmers separately, but hey, if you like the layered look, far be it from us to stop you!)

WHAT YOU'LL NEED
* sweater

TECHNIQUES YOU'LL NEED
* zigzag stitch

TIME TO COMPLETE
30 minutes

STEP 1: LAY IT FLAT

Lay your sweater out flat on the worksurface. Place your left hand down on the sweater so that your four fingers are touching each other, and your thumb is out to the side. (Think of the hand signal for "stop.")

Be conscious of where you are placing your hand on the sweater—the design underneath

your hand will be the design on your mitten.
If you want to make things easy on yourself,
line your hand up so that the bottom of the mitten is the bottom of the sweater. Then you won't
have to finish the edges—they're already done
for you! (See illustration above.)

Using some chalk or a pen, draw an outline
around your hand. You want to draw the outline
so it's about ½ inch bigger than your hand all the
way around. Now do the same with your right
hand. If you want the pattern on the mittens to
match, be sure to place your right hand on a
part of the sweater that matches the left. Another way to make your mittens match is to work
from a paper pattern that you cut ahead of time.

STEP 2: PIN IT TOGETHER

Pin the front and back sides of the sweater together somewhere inside the mitten lines you've
drawn. Going through both the front and back
layers of the sweater, cut the sweater on the
lines you just drew.

STEP 3: SEW IT UP

Face the party sides of the cut pieces together.
Using a zigzag stitch with a medium stitch
length and width, sew all the way around the cut
edges, being sure to leave the bottom of the
mitten open.

STEP 4: ARM WARMER TIME!

As a bonus project, take the remainder of the
sweater (or a new one if you used the arms to
make the mittens), and cut the sleeves off a
couple inches below the shoulder seam. Slide
your new arm warmer (the former sleeve of the
sweater) up your fabulous biceps and there you
have it! Warm limbs, cool lady.

Move Over, Buttons, Here Comes Something Better

We're going to take a long-sleeve, button-down shirt and turn it into a cute, versatile tank. Sift through those thrift racks and find yourself a button-down shirt, preferably a men's shirt with a square body. A women's button-down might work, but they're usually too small and fitted through the torso. More important, make sure you like the fabric. If it's scratchy, ugly, or just not your color, pass it by. And make sure all the buttons are intact. You'll need them to take full advantage of this movable-button tank!

WHAT YOU'LL NEED
* men's long-sleeve, button-down shirt (large or extra-large)

TECHNIQUES YOU'LL USE
* straight stitch
* topstitching
* darting
* hemming

TIME TO COMPLETE
1 hour

STEP 1: CUT OFF THE SLEEVES
This tank is made from the body section and sleeves of the shirt. First, unbutton the shirt. Cut off the sleeves and set them aside for later;

we'll make the straps with these pieces. Now cut open the shoulder seams so you have a flat piece of fabric to work with.

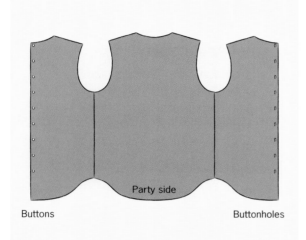

Buttons   Buttonholes

STEP 2: MAKE A GAME PLAN

Measurements You'll need to gather a few measurements before going any further: your bust measurement (the widest part around your chest), the desired length of your finished tank, and the length of your straps. You can take these measurements from your dress form or

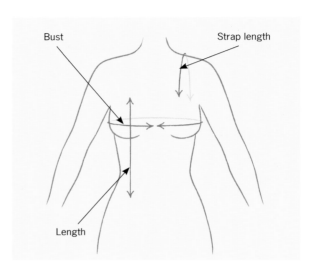

from your body, or perhaps you already have them written down from another project.

Front panel Now, take a look at the shirt you just cut open. The front panel of your new tank will be made from the front panel of the shirt with the buttons attached. (The buttons will run along the top of the new tank.) Cut a rectangular panel that spans the area from the armpit of the shirt to the hem, with the length equal to the desired length of the shirt (13 inches in our case), plus ½ inch for seam allowance (our front panel is 17 inches by 13½ inches).

Since you are using the button placket for the top of the tank, you don't have to hem it! Hooray!

Back panel In our example, our bust measurement was 36 inches. We added 4 inches for fit and 1 inch for seam allowance, bringing it to 41 inches total. The widest piece we could cut from the front of the shirt was 17 inches (as is the case with most extra-large shirts), so the back panel needs to be 24 inches wide. Orient the panel to use the existing shirt tail along the bottom edge. Remember to add a ½ inch to your length measurement for hemming the top edge. Our back panel is 24 inches by 13½ inches.

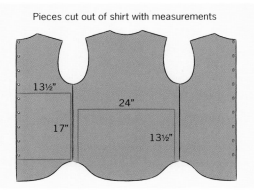

Pieces cut out of shirt with measurements

13½"

24"

17"

13½"

Straps The last pieces of your tank to consider are the straps. How wide do you want them to be? We decided on straps that will be 1½ inches wide. Accounting for ½ inch hem allowances we measured two strips of fabric that were 2½ inches wide.

Remember that one end of the strap will have a buttonhole and the other will need an extra ½ inch for seam allowance. Using the sleeves of the original shirt, we marked off two strips, each ending with a buttonhole, that were 2½ inches wide and 15½ inches long. We removed the existing button on each strap and snipped a buttonhole where the button used to live. (You don't need to sew around the buttonhole as this hole will tuck behind the preexisting buttonhole when you attach your sleeve to the shirt.)

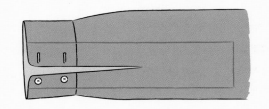

STEP 3: GET TO CUTTIN'

Now that you've planned, measured, and marked, it's time to cut it all out. Here are all of our pieces.

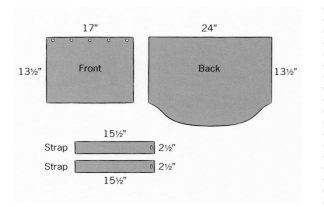

STEP 4: PUT IT TOGETHER

Top hem on the back panel Take the back panel to the ironing board, fold the top edge over ½ inch, and iron it. Take the back panel to your sewing machine and stitch the fold in place using a straight stitch with a medium stitch length.

Bottom hem on the front panel Take the front panel to the ironing board and iron down a ½-inch fold along the bottom edge, just like you

did with the top edge of the back panel. Sew this hemmed edge down using a straight stitch with a medium stitch length.

Sew the tube Now, face the party side of the front panel to the party side of the back panel and sew them together at the sides, using a straight stitch with a medium stitch length. You should have a tube of fabric now, with finished edges on all sides.

Hem the straps Finish the long edges by ironing a ½-inch fold down both sides of each strip. Topstitch these edges down using a straight stitch with a medium stitch length. Depending on the pattern of your fabric, you may want to use a zigzag or other decorative stitch here to add some flair. This is the time to take advantage of your fancy stitches and impress your friends!

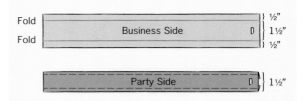

STEP 5: MAKE IT FIT

Slip the tube onto Ms. Trouble and button the straps onto the buttons on the front of the tube. Pin the straps to the back of the tube wherever you like and adjust the length as necessary. Isn't that cool? You're refashioning like a champ!

The tank should have a baggy fit and still be a little unflattering; you need to pin the spots to be taken in or darted. (For more on darting, see p. 26.)

We decided on two vertical darts down the back panel. To improve the fit of your new tank, you can add darts, pin tucks, or even use elastic to ruche the loose fabric.

Now that your tank is fitted, make sure the placement of your straps is still correct. If you need to move them, do so now, and sew them into place. Face the party side of the strap to the business side of the back panel, and stitch them to the tube using a straight stitch with a medium stitch length. Go over it a few times to make sure your stitches will not come loose.

Shimmy your way into your new tank and button yourself in. Button the straps straight

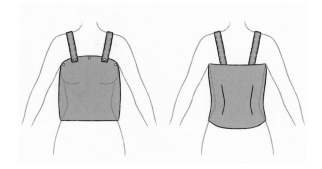

down, close together, out under your armpits, or cross them and get really crazy! We know how you are.

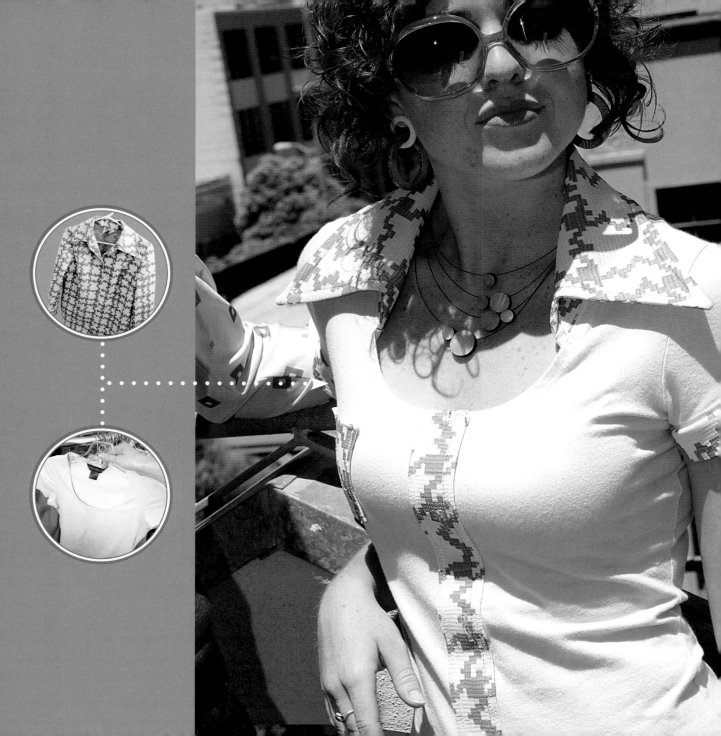

Ain't No Collar Back Girl!

So many shirts, so little time! We'll solve that problem by wearing more than one shirt at once! The racks at Sally's (aka Salvation Army) are filled with knit tees and cute, funky-print button-down shirts. Which one to wear? Wear them both! We mix our tee with a button-down polyester shirt. We're only going to use a portion of the polyester top, so don't worry if it's a little loud. In fact, the crazier, the better!

WHAT YOU'LL NEED

* plain, fitted knit top (preferably short-sleeved)
* collared, button-down polyester shirt

TECHNIQUES YOU'LL USE

* zigzag stitch

TIME TO COMPLETE

1½ hours

STEP 1: SHIRT SURGERY

Cut the collar off your polyester shirt, leaving about ½ inch of excess fabric attached to the collar for seam allowance. If your polyester shirt has a pocket, cut that off too (if not, and you still desire pockets, you can cut a piece of fabric off the shirt to fashion your own pocket).

Cut off the button placket (aka the strip of fabric with the buttonholes on it), leaving no excess. You need only the strip with the button-holes, not the side with the buttons. If the placket isn't hemmed on both sides of the buttonholes, cut a strip that is 2½ inches wide and finish the rough edge with a ½-inch hem.

Measure the circumference of each armhole on your knit shirt. Cut two 3-inch-wide strips of fabric out of the polyester shirt that match the

circumference measurement, plus 1 inch. On our shirt, the armholes are 11 inches around, so we cut two 3-inch by 12-inch strips of fabric from the polyester shirt.

If your knit shirt is long-sleeved, consider using the existing cuffs from the polyester shirt as the finishing for the sleeve. In this case, you'll want to leave ½ inch of excess fabric attached

to the cuffs for seam allowance, just as you did with the collar.

STEP 2: PINNING

Measure the length of your knit shirt from the center of the neckline to the bottom of the shirt.

Cut down your button placket to match this length, plus 1 inch to allow for a ½-inch hem at both the top and bottom of the shirt. Our knit shirt is 17 inches long, so we cut the button placket piece to be 18 inches long.

Fold the button placket piece over ½ inch at both ends and pin the piece to the front center of the shirt. (You are essentially folding over your hem instead of sewing.) Remember to pin perpendicular to the seam line!

STEP 3: TACK IT ON

Using a zigzag stitch with medium stitch width and medium stitch length, sew the button placket piece to the knit shirt by sewing down one side of the placket, and then down the other. Use the free arm on your machine and be sure not sew the front and back of the shirt together. Be careful to catch the folded ends in your sewing.

STEP 4: POCKET IT

With your shirt on your dress form or your body, pin the pocket you cut off earlier to your shirt. Sew the pocket on using the same zigzag stitch you were using earlier. If you make your own pocket, be sure to hem the edges first so they aren't raw and raggedy. Also, remember to leave the top of the pocket open. It sounds silly, but that mistake can happen to you!

STEP 5: COLLAR ME STYLISH

It's time to attach Ms. Collar to Ms. Knit Shirt. Find the center of the collar and the center of the neckline on the back of your knit shirt. Mark these spots with straight pins. Pin the collar to the inside of your knit shirt, matching up the centers.

Pin the collar all the way around the neckline of your knit shirt so the party side of the collar faces the business side of the knit shirt. Eventually, you will be sewing the ½ inch of excess fabric attached to the collar to your knit shirt, so pin accordingly.

Use a zigzag stitch with medium stitch width and medium stitch length to attach the collar to the shirt.

STEP 6: CUFF 'EM AND LEAVE 'EM

We're almost done! Now take those strips of fabric you cut out of the polyester shirt and fold them in half lengthwise, with business side facing business side (party side facing out, please!). Iron the fold flat and pin the strips around the circumference of the armholes on your knit shirt, with the party side facing the party side of the knit shirt, and the cut edges of the strip lined up with the edge of the sleeve. You should

Make a straight stitch, sewing open edge of folded strip to edge of sleeve.

have about ½ inch of overlap on the ends of the polyester strips. The overlap should live on the underside of your arm so it isn't as visible. Sew the strips in place with a straight stitch. Turn the strip out so the seam is on the inside, and iron the strip down flat.

That's it! Try on your funky new collared tee, and say goodbye to the days of boring solid knit tops! That was *so* 90 minutes ago.

make it your way

You can apply the same concepts using a turtleneck shirt in place of the polyester shirt. (Hint: A turtleneck split up the side becomes a mod neckline!) Get creative. Attach whatever parts of Shirt A that you like (say, sleeves) to Shirt B (the knit shirt).

Alternatively, you can remove the buttons from the original shirt and stitch them into the buttonholes on your new shirt! They won't be functional, but we can make that our little secret.

Put the "Olé!" in Your Bolero

Turtlenecks are a universal winter favorite. Not only do they keep you nice and toasty, but they frame your gorgeous face in the most flattering, adorable way. We're giving the piles of turtlenecks in the thrift stores their proper respect by extracting the cuteness from a turtleneck sweater and transforming it into the most adorable little bolero jacket this side of Madrid! You can make this bolero from any fitted sweater, but the turtleneck feature adds a great collar, so if you can find one, snatch it up.

WHAT YOU'LL NEED
* turtleneck sweater
* ⅔ yard of ribbon

TECHNIQUES YOU'LL USE
* lettuce edging

TIME TO COMPLETE
1 hour

STEP 1: MARK IT UP!

Slip the turtleneck onto your dress form and use a safety pin to mark a spot about 2 to 3 inches below your bust. (You can do this on yourself, but please be careful when pinning!) You are going to cut the sweater off at this mark, so be sure the length is right for you.

Use another safety pin to mark a spot on the sleeve 2 to 3 inches below your elbow. We'll be cutting the sweater at this mark to create a cute three-quarter-length sleeve.

STEP 2: CUT IT UP

Lay your sweater on a flat surface. Using a sharp pair of scissors, cut the sweater off in the middle of the bodice, then cut the sleeves off at your marked lines. (If you'd like, chalk your cutting lines first to be sure you are making a straight cut.) Save the extra pieces, as they make great arm warmers or wrist cuffs!

STEP 3: SWEATER SPLIT

Cut the sweater straight down the middle in the front, from the top of the turtleneck to the

bottom edge of the sweater.

Try your bolero on. The turtleneck is now a collar. Hot! Now's the time to make any last-minute length and sleeve adjustments before we embellish.

STEP 4: LETTUCE HAVE SOME FUN

Set your sewing machine to a zigzag stitch with a wide stitch width and a medium stitch length. Starting from the top left corner of the collar, sew a zigzag stitch around the cut edges of the sweater. Tug gently on the fabric before it goes under the needle to get that ruffle effect known as lettuce edging (see p. 18). Do the same with the cut edges of the sleeves. Try to the get your zigzag stitch as close to the edge of the fabric as possible.

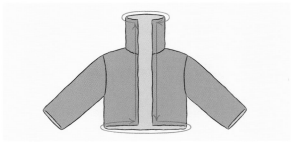

STEP 5: RIBBON IS OUR FRIEND

Try on your new bolero again. How cute are you? Hang in there! We just have one more step before you can head out for your salsa class. Place a pin on the lapels where you would like the bolero to close. Cut two 12-inch pieces of ribbon. Take the sweater off and sew the ribbon pieces to the bolero (by hand or machine), with one ribbon on each side of the bolero's opening. These ribbons will act as the closure.

STEP 6: SWEET, SWEET BOLERO

Don your new bolero sweater, tie the ribbons closed, and put some dancing shoes on. You're one hot tamale! Olé!

make it your way

If your sweater is loosely knit, try weaving a ¼-inch-wide ribbon through the holes along the edges instead of making the lettuce edge.

Launch Yo Poncho

Ponchos recently made a comeback after many years of style exile, but let's face it: They aren't the most practical items to wear (at least as they were originally intended). Alas, the poncho's shortcoming is your opportunity to create the perfect skirt! When searching the secondhand stores, look for a poncho that has an open knit or crochet stitch, with a neck hole large enough to fit around your waist. You can do this project with any kind of poncho, but one with a large, loose knit will bring out your best boho chic.

WHAT YOU'LL NEED
- knit poncho
- 2 yards of ribbon

TECHNIQUES YOU'LL USE
- zigzag stitch

TIME TO COMPLETE
1 hour

STEP 1: TRY IT ON

Start by turning the poncho inside out and pulling it up over your or Ms. Trouble's hips. If the poncho looks great as is, you're one lucky lady. You get to skip to step 4. More likely, the poncho is going to puff around the hips, or maybe it won't even fit around your waist at all.

STEP 2: EXCESS IS NOT ALWAYS BEST

Many ponchos are contoured near the neck-line so that they nicely follow the curve of your shoulders. We need to take out this curve so that the poncho follows the curve of your hips. With the poncho still on, use a few safety pins to take up the excess material around your hips (see p. 24 for more information on taking it in a notch).

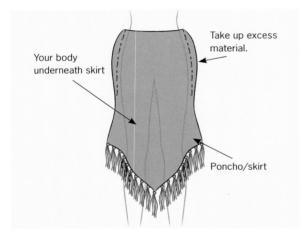

STEP 3: WAIST NOT

Since ponchos are designed to be worn around your neck, the neck hole may not fit over your hips or around your waist. If this is the case, cut off the neckband just below the top of the poncho. Fold over this cut edge and hem it using a straight stitch with medium stitch length.

STEP 4: DRAWSTRING IS KING

Grab your ribbon and put a safety pin through one end of it. Using the safety pin like a needle, thread the ribbon around the waist portion of the poncho.

Using a zigzag stitch with a medium width and length, sew the darts where you placed your pins. Try the skirt on again to make sure it hugs your curves in all the right places.

STEP 5: PONCHO-FY YOUR LOOK

Slip your new boho skirt on over a vintage slip or a patterned skirt and tie the drawstring ribbon. Find your biggest boho sunglasses and head to the flea market, you stylish girl!

Mandarin Collar, Puffy Sleeves, and Hoodie—Oh My!

We, the ladies of *Subversive Seamster*, love hoodies. The comfort, the flexibility, and the softness of a favorite hoodie makes us all warm and fuzzy inside and out! In this project, we dissect a thrift-store hoodie and transform it into a hip mandarin-collared jacket without sacrificing a bit of its comfort.

WHAT YOU'LL NEED
- hoodie

TECHNIQUES YOU'LL USE
- zigzag stitch
- pin tucks

TIME TO COMPLETE
2 hours

STEP 1: UNHOODIE-FY THE HOODIE

Trim the hood off your hoodie using a sharp pair of scissors. If possible, leave the finished edge on the jacket, not the hood (see p. 32 for more info on this technique).

Using the same technique, cut the sleeves off your jacket. Again, leave the finished edge on the jacket, not the sleeve.

STEP 2: PIN-TUCK LIKE THERE'S NO TOMORROW

In our sample, we sewed a series of pin tucks on the chest and back area of our jacket. (See p. 30 for instructions.) Not only does this look cool, but it makes the armholes a little smaller for a more fitted silhouette. (This is yet another technique that is flattering *and* adds extra cuteness.)

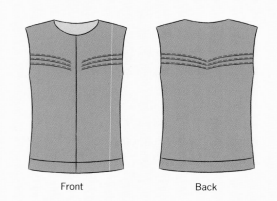

Front   Back

STEP 3: REATTACH THE ARMS

Before we reattached the sleeves to the jacket, we shortened the arms to a cute three-quarter-length sleeve. If you don't love the three-quarter-length as much as we do, you can leave your sleeves long.

For a three-quarter-length sleeve, cut the sleeve shorter on the rough end. When you cut, mimic the shape of the sleeve where it currently attaches to the jacket, so it will easily reattach in the next step. Our sleeve, for example, has an S-shape. Remember your shape by tracing it onto paper. (See our example in the illustration above.)

Now measure the distance from your shoulder to the place where you want your three-quarter-length sleeve to end. Add ½ inch to this measurement for seam allowance. For example, if the distance from your shoulder to below your elbow is 15 inches, mark a spot on the sleeve that is 15½ inches above the cuff.

Use your traced shape to chalk a line like the one in the illustration at left onto your sleeve. Cut the sleeve where you chalked your line.

Clever lady that you are, you must be wondering what we do now that the circumference of the armhole on the jacket is smaller than the circumference of the armhole on the sleeve. Don't worry! We've got a quick, cute fix for this. When you sew the sleeve back onto the jacket, start reattaching the sleeve at the armpit. By the time you get to the shoulder seam on the jacket, you can take up the excess by doing the ruffling technique we covered on p. 23. Not only does this take up the excess fabric, but now you've got yourself an adorable puffy-sleeved jacket!

Depending on how long your sleeves were to begin with, you may not have cut them off. This means no reattaching (hooray!), but you will miss out on your puffy sleeve. It's your call!

STEP 4: MEASURE THE NECKLINE AND CUT A STRIP

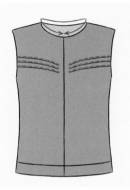

Now that the sleeves are reattached, it's time to work on the mandarin collar. First, measure the circumference of the neckline.

Cut a strip of fabric from the hood that is the length of your neckline measurement and 5 inches wide. Fold the strip in half lengthwise with the party side facing the party side. You should end up with a strip of fabric that is 2½ inches wide and as long as your neckline.

Using a straight stitch with a long stitch length and leaving the cut side open, sew a gentle curve on your fabric. This gives you a rounded mandarin collar instead of a square one.

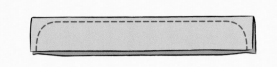

Trim off the fabric around your stitch line, leaving about ⅜ inch excess, and turn your strip right-side out again.

Locate the center of your strip by folding it in half. Find the back center of your neckline and mark it with a pin. Matching the centers of the neckline and the strip, pin the strip inside the jacket so that the party side of the strip faces the business side of the jacket. Using a straight stitch with a long stitch length, sew the strip to the jacket.

make it your way

To give your new mandarin-collared shirt a little more mandarin flair, add a frog (the ball-and-loop-type closure often seen on mandarin collared shirts).

Get Your Giddyup On

There's a little bit of cowgirl in each of us just screaming to ride off into the sunset. We yearn to be wild women of the West—or at least dress like them—with their fabulous boots, belt buckles, and hats. And every good cowgirl needs a good cowgirl shirt! Even if you have never sat on a horse, with the help of two handy-dandy button-down shirts, you too can be an urban Annie Oakley. For this project, we'll wed two unsuspecting shirts into one western wearable. Both shirts should be woven, as knits can give you trouble. The first shirt should be plain and should somewhat match the color scheme of the second shirt. The second shirt can be as wild as you like, as long as the shoulder measurements are similar in width to those of the plain shirt. (This project works really well with a fitted women's button-down.)

WHAT YOU'LL NEED

* button-down shirt (men's or women's)
* loud Hawaiian shirt, polyester shirt, or otherwise funky patterned shirt (stretchy shirts can be used, but know they are a little harder to work with because of all that stretchy goodness)

TECHNIQUES YOU'LL USE

* topstitching

TIME TO COMPLETE

1 hour

STEP 1: SNIP OFF THE SLEEVES AND COLLAR

Remove the sleeves and collar from your funky print shirt and turn it inside out. Put the plain shirt on your dress form (or over the back of a chair) and layer the new sleeveless shirt on top, party side to party side. (You are not going to sew it this way, but you'll be marking on it, so it's best to turn it inside out, just to be safe.)

Remove sleeves and collar.

STEP 2: GET YOUR POINT ACROSS

Determine the pattern you'd like your cowgirl shirt to have on the shoulders and the back. Traditional cowgirl shirts have a V-shaped point on each side of the chest, and a big one in the back. Trace the shape you want on your shirt.

Place pieces on top of plain shirt.

STEP 3: CUT 'EM UP, LADY

Remove the patterned shirt from the dress form or chair back and cut out the shapes with a ½-inch seam allowance. Iron the seam allowance under and place your shirt pieces back on the plain shirt (business side to party side). Pin it into place and try it on, making sure everything looks hunky-dory.

Front

Back

Plain

Funky

STEP 4: SEW COWGIRL!

Using a zigzag stitch with a medium stitch length and width, sew the print fabric onto your button-down shirt so that every edge is tacked down. Try your shirt on and admire your fine country looks. Yee-haw!

make it your way

Advanced cowgirls can add matching (or contrasting, if you like) bias tape to the edges of the patterned shirt before sewing it down to give it a real cowgirl piping look. Add any remaining piping to the wrists for a little more flair. If you want to get authentic, look for some similarly sized pearl buttons from a not-as-cute (clearly!) cowboy shirt on the racks.

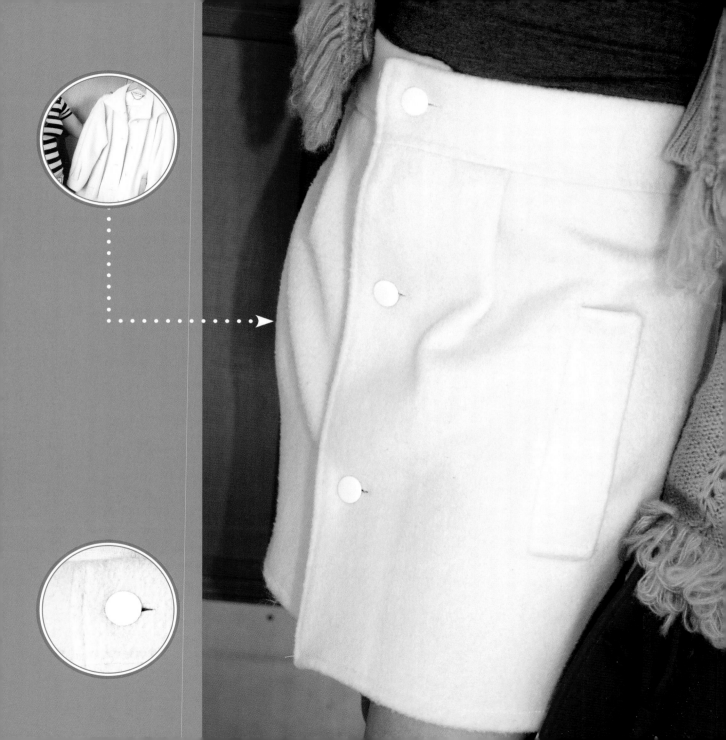

Wooly Bully Winter Skirt

A tired and out-of-date wool jacket gives life to a fresh and stylish winter skirt. Just throw on some tights with your favorite boots, and you will be the stylin' girl around town this winter! Start with a jacket that is fitted at the bottom and baggy around the torso, one with a band at the bottom and preferably with buttons. (We'll show you how to deal with a zipper, too.) Don't feel the need to limit yourself to wool. Be as adventurous as your local thrift shop will allow! Try using a leather jacket (as long as your sewing machine can handle it) to rock your serious hotness.

WHAT YOU'LL NEED
* wool jacket with a waistband and buttons

TECHNIQUES YOU'LL USE
* taking in
* topstitching
* straight stitch
* hemming

TIME TO COMPLETE
45 minutes

STEP 1: CUT YOUR SKIRT OUT

For a sneak preview, turn the jacket upside down! The band that would have gone over your hips (yuck!) will now sit comfortably at your waist (hooray!). Cut a straight line from armpit to armpit, discarding the sleeves, shoulders, and neck. Eureka! You've discovered a skirt!

STEP 2: SIZE IT RIGHT

You may need to size down the waistband of your skirt. Use your dress form or a full-length

Side view of skirt

Skirt too big

mirror to size it properly.

Take in the back seam to fit your waist and hips and to minimize bulk along the side seams. Use a

straight stitch with a medium stitch length and cut away any excess fabric to make the skirt less bulky.

After you've taken in the seam, topstitch each side of the seam to make the seam lie flat and to minimize bulk in the back of the skirt.

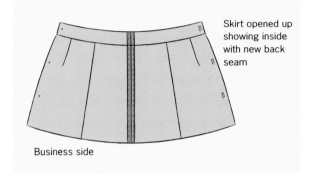

Skirt opened up showing inside with new back seam

Business side

STEP 3: CLOSURE CHECK

If your jacket has buttons, make sure they are all sewn on tightly and do not need to be reattached. If the buttons are far apart enough to have some gaps in "coverage," and you need to add buttons to keep your skirt together, now's the time.

If your jacket had a zipper, sew the zipper

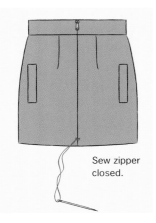

Sew zipper
closed.

closed (by sewing back and forth over the teeth a few times) about ½ inch above the cut bottom edge of the skirt. You should do this by hand so that you don't break a needle trying to sew over the zipper on your machine. Make sure the teeth stay tightly closed, so the zipper doesn't come off and separate the teeth.

STEP 4: FINISH IT UP

The last thing to do is hem the bottom edge of the skirt. Fold down a ½-inch hem and pin it. Topstitch with a straight stitch of medium stitch length.

Wear this wooly bully winter skirt with vintage stacked-heel boots, and add tights if your office doesn't have a heater.

BOTTOMS UP!

☆ Suburban Pants, Meet City Shorts

☆ Salsa, Not Just for Chips Anymore

☆ Peek-a-Bootylicious Skirt

☆ Good Girls Gone Tank

☆ Busting Out of Old-Man Pants

☆ That Really Chaps My Gauchos

☆ Always a Bridesmaid, Never a Tie
   (or Halter)

☆ Hot Muumuu Mama

☆ Less Rock, More Rack!

Every season brings a whole slew of new pants and dresses. While the trends might be a pain for those buying ready-to-wear, it's a plus for the ready-to-refashion seamster. You should be able to find a number of last year's pants to turn into stylin' bustiers, shorts, and skirts. The "I'll never wear-it-again" bridesmaids' gowns make fabulous ties and halters. Rockin '80s dresses can be reincarnated as corsets. Don't forget about muumuus! Their prints and yardage can be your fashion canvas. Take those fashion has-beens and turn them into refashioned must-haves.

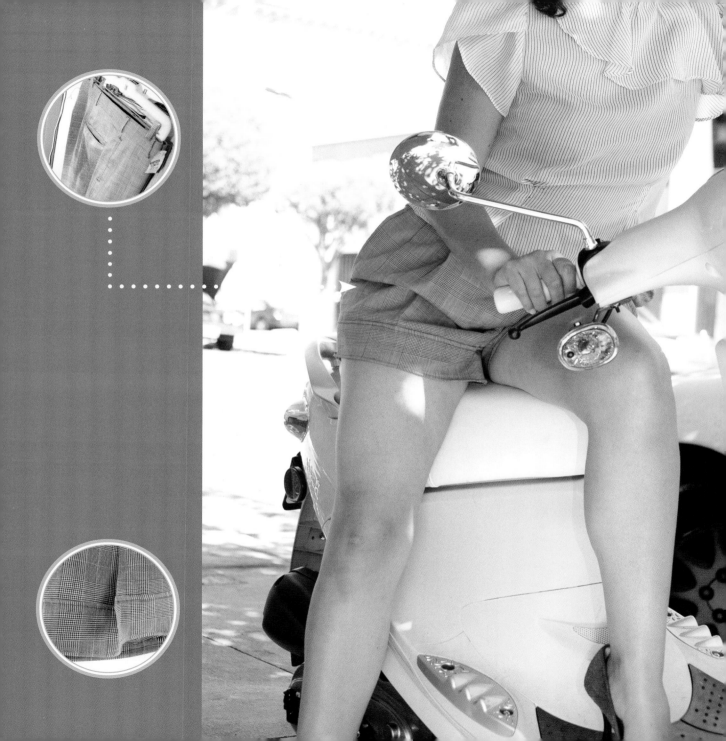

Suburban Pants, Meet City Shorts

Cuffed city shorts are all the rage on the red carpet. Sift through the piles of fancy work pants at your local thrift shop to find a pair that fits your shape well. Look for pants with a loose fit; remember that they will eventually be shorts, so it's OK to go against everything we've ever said and buy a pair of (gasp) tapered pants. (Just don't make a habit of it!)

WHAT YOU'LL NEED
* pants

TECHNIQUES YOU'LL USE
* straight stitch

TIME TO COMPLETE
1 hour

STEP 1: PLAN, PLAN, PLAN

Before we get started, think about how long you want your finished shorts to be. Do you err on the side of short, or are you more of a modest lady? How tall do you want the cuff to be? We went for 12 inches above the knee and a modest 1-inch cuff. (At least our cuff is modest!)

STEP 2: GET TO CUTTIN'

Cut off your slacks at the desired length (somewhere above the knee), plus two times the height of your cuff you want and an additional ½ inch for hemming. After all that calculating, we cut our slacks 9½ inches above the knee.

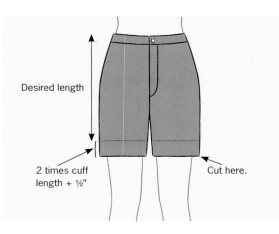

Desired length

2 times cuff length + ½"

Cut here.

Fold and iron line 1, business side to business side, then fold and iron line 2, party side to party side

2

1

STEP 3: CUFF ME

To set the cuff in place, fold the hemmed edge under to the desired height of your cuff plus ½ inch for seam allowance, business side to business side, and iron it in place. Now fold the ironed edge up to the desired height of the cuff, and iron this in place. At this point, the cuff should look the way you want when you're wearing it. If it's not right, just iron out your folds and start over again.

When the folds look just right, sew the cuff into place by topstitching all the way around the cuff, or by hand-tacking it in a few places.

If you have thinner fabric, you'll want to topstitch all the way around so that the folds don't come undone when you're jumping around in your hot little shorts.

Stitch around... ...or tack strategically.

STEP 4: STRUT YOUR STUFF!

Get your fancy shorts on and work it, city girl! Try glamming up your city shorts by belting them with 1-inch shiny ribbon, laced though the belt loops and tied in a bow.

Salsa, Not Just for Chips Anymore

Every girl needs a nice, sensible A-line skirt in her closet. But let's face it, plain A-line skirts aren't the most exciting thing to wear, so a lot of them end up at Goodwill, just ripe for the pickin'. With a little bit of creativity and some fabric dye, you can take that A-line skirt from sensible to sizzling! In this project, we show you how to add a little Latin flavor to a plain white skirt by using a bold new color and tiered ruffles. You can use any skirt that fits you well around the hips and waist for this project, and you'll want something with a little bit of length, hitting you around midcalf.

WHAT YOU'LL NEED

- skirt
- fabric dye (optional)
  —we used Rit® Dye Liquid

TECHNIQUES YOU'LL USE

- dyeing (optional)
- ruffling
- straight stitch
- fabric flower (optional)

TIME TO COMPLETE

2 hours (3 hours if dyeing)

To Dye For

Don't feel the need to limit yourself to skirts that can be dyed. If you are planning on dyeing your fabric, however, be sure to find a skirt that is made out of cotton, linen, silk, wool, rayon, nylon, or acetate (or any blends that contain more than 50 percent of one of these fibers). Fabrics containing 50 percent or more polyester won't take the dye well. To be sure, always check the dye package or manufacturer's website for recommended fabric types.

STEP 1 (OPTIONAL): I'M DYEING TO REFASHION THIS SKIRT!

Before we even get near the sewing machine, we'll need to dye our skirt. We ♥ dyeing! It's incredibly satisfying to transform a boring item of clothing by punching in some bright color. Let's get started: Follow the instructions on p. 33 and let your blah color blossom into something vibrant!

STEP 2: SIZE MATTERS

Now that you've pumped up the color from basic to *bueno*, it's time to make the style match the hue. Try the skirt on and use a safety pin to mark a spot 4 inches above your desired hem length. Take off the skirt, lay it nice and flat on the floor or a table, and cut the bottom of the skirt off where you placed your pin.

STEP 3: STRIPSTER HIPSTER

Using all the excess fabric from the bottom  of the skirt, cut as many 4-inch-wide strips as the piece allows. Make sure the ends of the strips cut so they're squared off.

STEP 4: RUFFLES ARE NOT JUST CHIPS

Measure the circumference of the new bottom hem of your skirt. Double that measurement and sew together as many 4-inch-wide strips of fabric as you need to equal that measurement in length. For a fuller ruffle, just triple or quadruple the circumference measurement.

Since you are making a tiered ruffle, you will need a minimum of two of these 4-inch-wide strips.

Pin and sew the first strip to the bottom hem using a straight stitch with a medium stitch length, ruffling along the way. (See p. 23 for ruffling techniques.) Pin the top of the second strip to the skirt 1½ inches above the top of the bottom ruffle. Sew this strip down, again using a straight stitch with a medium stitch length, ruffling all the way home. Repeat this process with any remaining strips. Now slip into your sexy new salsa skirt and grab your castanets!

make it your way

A ROSE BY ANY OTHER NAME

If you have any excess fabric, follow the instructions on p. 16 to make a fabric flower. Add some spice by safety-pinning the flower onto your new skirt or a handbag!

FUNK IT UP

In step 2, cut the hem so that it is asymmetrical—cut the front shorter than the back, or the left side shorter than the right.

GET EXTRA RUFFLICIOUS

Instead of doing a tiered ruffle all the way around your hem, cut your strips into shorter segments and make tiered ruffles all the way up the length of the skirt. You can tier the ruffles up the center front or sew them on the center back of your skirt for a faux bustle effect.

Peek-a-Bootylicious Skirt

The main material for this skirt comes from an old pair of men's slacks with a pleated top. You know, the slacks that *used* to be cool, but now induce bubbles on the front of even the slimmest of people. Release the slacks' potential by cutting them up and adding a girly touch. For this project, you'll also need to find a lacy dress. Think '80s, first communion, *quinceñera*, homecoming, or prom. Try to look past the dated style of the dress and concentrate on the lace.

WHAT YOU'LL NEED
* pleated men's slacks
* lacy dress

TECHNIQUES YOU'LL USE
* straight stitch

TIME TO COMPLETE
45 minutes

STEP 1: CUT UP THE SLACKS

The first and easiest part of this project is to cut the legs off the slacks. Cut a straight line, just below the zipper.

STEP 2: TACKLE THOSE PLEATS!

Use a straight stitch with a medium stitch length to tack down the pleats in the top of the slacks.

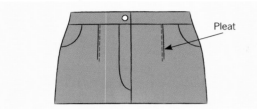

STEP 3: THE LACE SPACE

Measure the circumference of the cut edge of the slacks. Decide how long you want your skirt to be and measure the height of the existing top piece of the slacks. The top portion of our slacks were 8 inches in length, and we wanted our skirt to be 15 inches long from waist to hem. Using the lacy dress, cut a strip of lace that is equal to the circumference of the cut edge of the slacks (plus 1 inch for seam allowance) and the height of your desired skirt minus the height of the slacks portion. Be sure to add ½ inch for seam allowance and another ½ inch if you want to hem the lace strip. In our sample,

we didn't need not to hem the lace strip, so our cut strip was 15 inches – 8 inches + ½ inch = 7½ inches in height.

Using a straight stitch with a medium stitch length, sew the lace strip all the way around the bottom of the cut slacks top. If you want to hem your strip, be sure to do so *before* you sew the strip on to the skirt. It's not the end of the world if you hem it afterward—it's just easier to sew the hem when the piece is unattached.

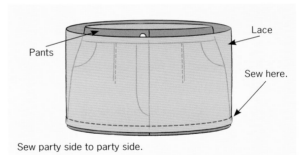

Sew party side to party side.

STEP 4: THE PANEL CHANNEL

We're almost done! We decided on four panels around the skirt. Before you start cutting, you need to figure out the dimensions of your panels.

Start by dividing the circumference of the cut edge of the slacks by 4. The circumference of our slacks was 40 inches, so we determined that our panels had to be 10 inches wide plus 1 inch for each of the side hems (½ inch each), which equals 11 inches wide. Using the leftover fabric from the pant legs you cut off previously, cut four panels to this newly measured width and cut them to the same height as your lace strip. We decided to hem the bottom of our panels (though we didn't hem the bottom of our lace strip), so we added ½ inch to the height of the panel. We ended up with four panels that were 11 inches wide by 8 inches tall.

Start hemming your panels by folding and ironing down ½-inch folds on three sides of the panels. Sew down the folds using a straight stitch with medium stitch length. Now, pin the unhemmed edge of the panels to the bottom of the slacks top, party side to party side, exactly where you sewed the lace strip onto the slacks. We placed the panels so that the first panel was centered on the zipper. While you don't have to do that, you might want to, because you will be showing some skin where the panels meet, and you don't want to overexpose yourself. Pinning the front panel so that its center lines up with the zipper ensures that you will remain a lady (albeit one hot lady!).

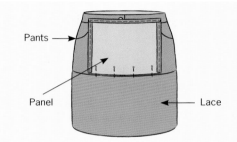

Pin the rest of the panels onto the skirt.

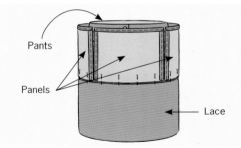

Using a straight stitch with a medium stitch length, sew the panels onto the cut edge of the slacks. *Voila!* You've got a peek-a-boo skirt that shows off your best assets!

Good Girls Gone Tank

As soon as summer rolls around, school uniforms can be found aplenty in the thrift stores. Snatch one up for yourself and transform that plaid, pleated schoolgirl skirt into a fitted, strapless, classy-lady top. The waistband of the skirt needs to fit around your chest (above the Girls, under the armpits), and that's about it. Buy your skirt based on the plaid. Are you a red-green-blue-white gal or a multiple-shades-of-blue gal?

WHAT YOU'LL NEED
* pleated schoolgirl uniform skirt

TECHNIQUES YOU'LL USE
* topstitching
* taking in
* working it

TIME TO COMPLETE
30 minutes

STEP 1: CLOSE UP THE PLEATS, PLEASE

The first step to form-fitting your top is to stitch down those unflattering pleats. To allow for some extra breathing room, we left the bottom

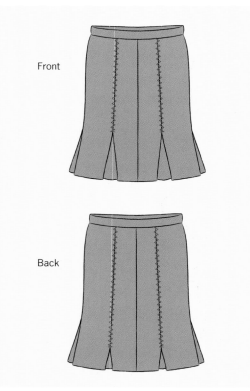

Front

Back

portions of the pleats open on the front and the back and a little more on the front side to accentuate the bust. (We're no dummies!)

STEP 2: FIT YOUR FORM

Slip the top onto Ms. Trouble (or on yourself) and pin any areas that need to be taken in. We had to take in the side seams and add two darts in the back (see p. 26 for more on darting) for shaping. To keep this project easy, start at the side seam opposite the zipper and sew a seam straight from the waistband to the hem. On the side with the zipper, sew a seam from the end of the zipper straight down to the hem. Do most of your taking in with the darts in the back. If your skirt is plaid (and most of them are), try to match the pattern when you're pinning to make it blend as much as possible (unless you're into the vertigo thing).

Now squeeze yourself into this naughty little number with a pair of slim jeans or a pencil skirt, and hit us with your hotness one more time!

Busting Out of Old-Man Pants

Old-man pants, with their high waists, polyester feel, and funky patterning, are in abundance in thrift stores. As pants for fellow fashionistas, they are all wrong, but we'll show you how to make them all right! Take those pants and turn them into a sexy new bustier that hugs all the right curves! It's a good idea to start this project with a pair of pants that have the same waist measurement as your bust. For example, if you are 36 inches around the widest area of your bust, you want a pair of pants with a 36-inch waist. Also, this project is much easier to fit if you find a pair of polyester pants—the stretch in this material will work to your advantage!

WHAT YOU'LL NEED
* old-man pants

TECHNIQUES YOU'LL USE
* darting
* topstitching

TIME TO COMPLETE
1½ hours

STEP 1: LAY IT OUT

Lay the pants out flat on your worksurface. Cut the pants off right underneath the zipper and put the leg portion of the pants to the side. We'll be using this later.

STEP 2: DART MANIA

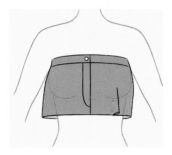

Slip the zippered portion of the pants onto Ms. Trouble inside out, so that the waistband is right over the top of her boobs. Pinch a bit of the excess fabric from the center of her boobs to the cut edge of the pants so that the Girls are cupped comfortably. Just be sure to leave a few extra inches of breathing room! Use a few safety pins to mark how much fabric you'll take in. (This can also be done with the help of a trusted friend if you haven't had time to make Ms. Trouble yet.)

Remove the piece from Ms. Trouble and set your sewing machine to a straight stitch with medium stitch length. Make darts by sewing a seam where you placed your safety pins (see p. 26 for more on darting).

STEP 3: MIDRIFF MAMA

This bustier is made up of the top portion of the pants (which you just fit over your bust) and a tubular piece that covers your midriff. Decide where you want to attach the midriff piece to the top portion of the pants. If you are a voluptuous lady, you might want to attach the midriff directly to the bottom of your bust piece. However, if your assets are a little more modest, you might want to pin the bottom piece a little higher up.

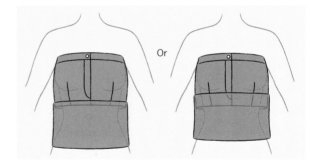

Notice that if you do pin the midriff piece a little higher up, you will have to sew over the zipper on the bust portion of the shirt. Since breaking needles is not subversive, go slowly when you get close to the zipper; when you're about 1 inch away from the zipper, pick up your presser foot, skip over the zipper, put your presser foot back down again, and continue stitching. You can tack the unsewn portion down by hand using a running stitch.

Now, measure the circumference of the bust portion at the point where you want to attach your midriff piece. This measurement is the bust circumference.

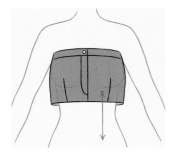

Now put the bust portion on the dress form again and measure from the spot where you will be attaching the midriff piece to your waist, or where you would like your bustier to end. Add 1 inch to this measurement for hemming and seam allowance. This is the midriff measurement.

STEP 4: GIVE PIECE A CHANCE

Use the fabric from the pant legs to piece together a portion of fabric that has a length equal to the bust circumference and a width equal to the midriff measurement. You may have to sew a few pieces of the pant legs together to end up with a piece of fabric with these measurements.

STEP 5: TOTALLY TUBULAR

Pin the midriff piece to the pants top with the party side facing the party side. Starting at one of the side seams, sew the midriff piece to the pants top, being careful to skip over the zipper if you need to. Then sew the midriff piece down the side seam so the midriff is now a tube.

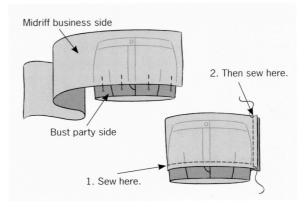

Midriff business side

2. Then sew here.

Bust party side

1. Sew here.

If you skipped over the zipper, now is the time to secure that spot using a hand needle and a simple running stitch.

STEP 6: OVER-THE-SHOULDER BOULDER HOLDER

OK, just one more task—the straps! Put the bustier on Ms. Trouble. Place a pin on the right front side of the bustier where you want the strap to be attached. Do the same on the left front, left back, and right back of the bustier. Using your measuring tape, measure from the right front safety pin to the right back safety pin. Cut two strips of fabric to that length and about 5 inches wide. If you want your straps to be wider or narrower, now's the time to branch out.

STEP 7: STRAPIFY

Fold the strips in half lengthwise with the party side facing the party side. Sew a seam straight down the length of the cut edge, using a ½-inch seam allowance.

Now turn the straps right-side out again. This can be tricky. If you're having trouble, try pinning a big safety pin on one end to hold as you feed it through the tube. Use an iron to flatten the straps out so that the seam you just stitched is in the center of the strap.

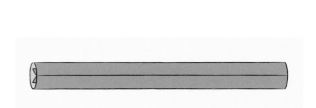

Now topstitch a line about ¼ inch from the right edge of each strap. Do the same on the left edge. This will make your straps lie flat.

STEP 8: STRAP IT ON

Pin your straps to the bustier where you placed your safety pins. Be sure to orient the straps so that the side with the seam line will eventually be facing your skin. Sew the straps on.

STEP 9: CHECK IT OUT

Put on your bustier and look in the mirror. I would dare someone to be hotter than you! For an extra-sexy look, undo the fly on the pants top for a plunging neckline! Naughty! We like it.

That Really Chaps My Gauchos

For this project, scour the racks to find a bargain pair of pants made from medium-weight woven fabric, but not from denim, silk, or satin. You want these pants to fit loosely and have a flat front. No pleats, please! Your pants can have any type of closure, and pockets are fine as long as they lie flat. You'll also need some cute flannel pj's to use for the fabric—we favor a good plaid pattern. You can even get away with a flannel sheet or a good-sized pillowcase.

WHAT YOU'LL NEED
* medium-weight pants
* cutely patterned flannel pj's

TECHNIQUES YOU'LL USE
* topstitching
* zigzag stitch

TIME TO COMPLETE
45 minutes

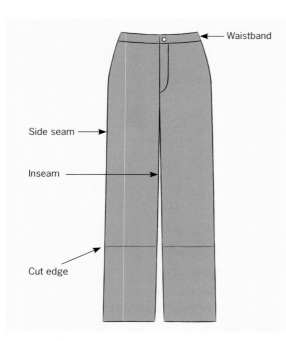

Waistband

Side seam

Inseam

Cut edge

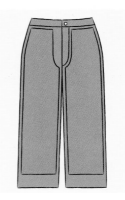

STEP 1: THE GAUCHO, THE CHAP, AND THE BLOOMER

Cut the pants off at the knees, or slightly below.

Using the flannel fabric from the pj's, cut two mirror-image pieces to fit on the front panels of the pants. The panels should reach from the side seam to the inseam and from the waistband to the cut edge. Use the illustrations above and at right as a guide for the shape.

STEP 2: SEW ON THE CHAPS

Pin the chaps on the front panels of the pants. Use a zigzag stitch with a medium stitch length and a wide stitch width to topstitch the chaps into place.

Pants front

This part is tricky because you must sew only on one side of the already constructed pants. Make things easier on yourself by using the free arm of your machine. Take your time! Reposition and check the fabric often to ensure that you aren't sewing the pants shut. If you have front pockets on your pants, you may be forced to sew them closed. We had to sew our pockets shut, but with pants as cute as these, we're over it!

Tip

If you want to make things easier on yourself here, you can cut or seam-rip the pants along the inseams so that the pants will lie flat under the machine. You'll have to sew them up again afterward, but it is easier to sew panels onto a flat piece of fabric than onto a pair of pants that are already constructed.

Always a Bridesmaid, Never a Tie (or Halter)

There are no two words like *bridesmaid's dress* to strike fear into the heart of any young lass (except maybe *swimsuit season*). Many bridesmaid dresses are notoriously, um, unfortunate. For this project, we take that satiny nightmare and give it a second chance by transforming it into the hottest little halter top and tie combo this side of Studio 54. You will need some extra fabric to complete this project, so when you hit Goodwill, look for a stretchy top in contrasting fabric. As for the bridesmaid's dress, you may even be able to raid your closet instead of the thrift shop. Get ready to rock it, bridesmaid style.

WHAT YOU'LL NEED

❋ bridesmaid's dress
(or another such unflattering satin dress—prom, winter formal, etc.)

FOR THE TIE

❋ old tie you like the shape and size of

FOR THE HALTER

❋ stretchy knit top in contrasting fabric
❋ chalk

TECHNIQUES YOU'LL USE

❋ hand stitch (tie)
❋ zigzag stitch (halter)

TIME TO COMPLETE

1 hour (tie)
1 hour (halter)

STEP 1: GET YOUR FABRIC TOGETHER

To start both projects, cut the dress down the seams or in the best way to preserve the longest piece of continuous fabric. (We find empire-waist dresses to be especially helpful in providing lots of fabric.) We'll start with the tie project, as it uses more fabric than you'd think.

STEP 2: OLD TIE SURGERY

Cut the old tie open down the back seam, being careful to save the inner piece of fabric that provides the structure. Unfold the old tie and iron it so it lies flat. Use this as a pattern and set it on the dress fabric. We like to lay the tie so that the weave of the fabric will be diagonal across the tie instead of straight up and down (this is

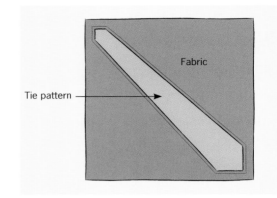

Tie pattern

Fabric

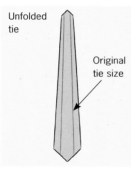

Unfolded tie

Original tie size

also known as cutting the fabric on the bias). Using chalk or a pen, trace around the tie pattern, adding a ½-inch seam allowance on all sides. Cut along the line you just drew.

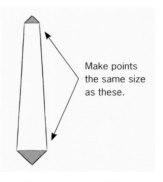

Make points the same size as these.

STEP 3: MAKE YOUR POINT

Cut two triangles matching the size of the ends of the tie. Add ½ inch for seam allowance.

Facing party side to party side, sew the triangles to each respective end of the tie. Turn them right-side out and poke out each tip with the end of a pen (capped, please!) so its point is sharpened. Iron the top of the tie to ensure a crisp corner.

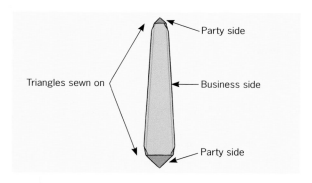

STEP 4: STURDY YOURSELF

Tuck the insert of the old tie into the fat end of the new tie. (The insert should be a somewhat rectangular, stiff piece of material that adds a little heft to the tie.) Tuck the insert into the small end of the tie and tack it in place with a couple of hand stitches.

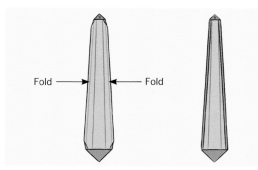

STEP 5: FOLD AND FINISH

Fold both raw edges of the new tie in (business side to business side) ½ inch and iron them down.

Fold again, slightly overlapping the two newly ironed edges by about ½ inch, and pin all your folds down. (This should now start to look like a bona fide tie!) When pinning, be careful not to push the pins all the way through the front of the new tie, as satin will show the pinholes, and that is not the subversive look we're going for!

STEP 6: SEW IT ALL TOGETHER NOW!

Hand-stitch down the center of the back of the tie, being careful to stitch only the two back sides together, not the front. If you occasionally

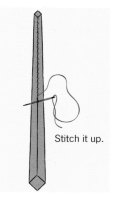

Stitch it up.

catch the stiff tie form in your stitch, that's OK, just make sure not to catch the front of the tie. Iron and serve to your favorite tie wearer! Now for the halter top . . .

STEP 1: NAVEL GAZING

Start off by measuring around your bust, and also from your collarbone to your belly button. Write these two measurements down somewhere, as you will be using them to cut your pieces.

STEP 2: CHALK AND CHOP

Slip the knit top onto Ms. Trouble. Using some chalk or pins, mark a line across her back that extends from underneath her left armpit to underneath her right.

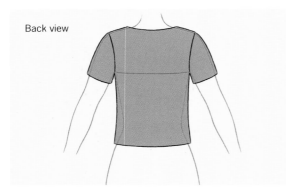

Back view

Undress Ms. Trouble and use a sharp pair of scissors to cut your knit top along the line you just marked and down the sides of the shirt,

making sure to cut off all excess fabric from your panel. Cut a long strip of fabric from the middle front panel of your knit top.

Lay the leftover material from the bridesmaid's dress out on a flat surface. You'll be cutting into the skirt portion of the dress, so be sure that area is nice and smooth. Cut out a rectangle of fabric from the dress that is as tall as the measurement from your collarbone to your waist and half as wide as your bust measurement. In other words, if your bust measurement is 36 inches and the length from your collarbone to your waist is 22 inches, cut out a rectangle that is 22 inches high by 18 inches wide. If, after making the tie, you don't have a complete piece in the size you need, improvise! The back of a skirt might have a flare and not lie flat, but turn that flare upside down, and you'll have a lovely draping neckline!

You should now have three pieces of fabric.

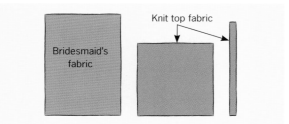

Knit top fabric

Bridesmaid's fabric

STEP 3: PIN ME

Facing party side to party side, line up the bottom edge of the knit top piece with the bottom edge of the bridesmaid's dress piece. Pin the pieces together along the side seams.

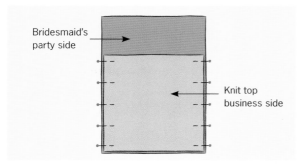

Bridesmaid's party side

Knit top business side

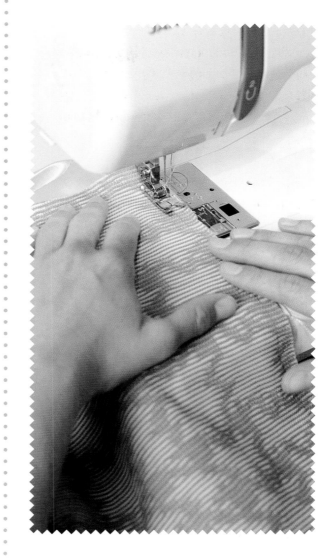

STEP 4: SEW EASY

Using a zigzag stitch with a medium stitch length and width, sew the seams that you just pinned.

Buttonholes

Bridesmaid party side

Now set your machine to make a buttonhole (see p. 27) and sew a buttonhole at each top corner of the bridesmaid dress fabric. Snip the buttonholes open.

STEP 5: TYING THE KNOT

Now it's time to put it all together. Using the strip of fabric you cut from the knit top, tie one end through the left buttonhole of the brides-

maid's dress fabric and the other end through the right buttonhole. Slip the top on over your head and adjust the knots, if necessary, so that the halter drapes across your

cleavage in the most flattering way possible. You may need to cut away excess fabric if your strip is too long.

Who cares if you're always the bridesmaid and never the bride when you can look this good?

Tip

Use leftover elements of the dress to make perfectly matching accessories. Cut out the skirt lining, hem it into a rectangle, and you've got a great shawl or scarf. Remove those covered buttons, string them on a wire, attach an earring blank, and you have dangly earrings! Or glue extra buttons to cuff-link findings and give a pair to your man to match his tie. The possibilities are endless! Waste nothing!

Hot Muumuu Mama

How often has your eye been caught by a bold, funky pattern in a thrift shop only to find that the print belongs to—ugh!—a muumuu? Well, despair no more, fair bargain maiden! Choose a muumuu with a print you really like and don't worry if it fits you like a potato sack—you'll make it into a peasant top that accentuates your finest features.

WHAT YOU'LL NEED

❋ muumuu
❋ 2 yards of ⅛-inch elastic

TECHNIQUES YOU'LL USE

❋ ruching

TIME TO COMPLETE

2 hours

STEP 1: PIN MARKS THE SPOT

Start by trying the muumuu on, using either yourself or Ms. Trouble as a model. Mark a spot just below your bust with a safety pin. Use another safety pin to mark the length of your shirt. Add 3 inches to 4 inches to your desired length, the ruching we do in this project will make the shirt ride up a bit. (You can always cut it shorter later if it is too long.) If you want to hem the bottom of your top, add another ½ inch to your desired length.

STEP 2: ROCK THE CHALK

Take the muumuu off and turn it inside out. Lay it down on a flat surface and use some chalk to draw two lines across the width of the shirt, where the pins are placed.

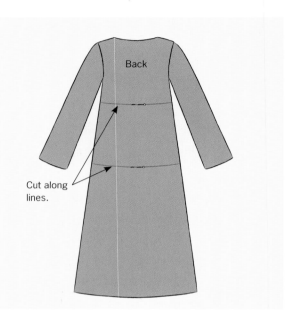

Back

Cut along
lines.

STEP 3: CUT IT OFF AND DON'T
LOOK BACK

Cut along the bottom line. Be sure that you have accounted for the seam allowance if you are hemming this edge.

If you are going to hem the bottom edge, now's the time. Fold the bottom edge under, business side to business side, so that the cut edge is facing the inside of the shirt. If you'd like, you can iron this fold down, though muu-muus are typically made of polyester, and polyester doesn't like to listen to Mr. Iron. (If you do use an iron, use a low heat setting—high heat and synthetic materials don't play well together.) Sew the fold down to set the hem using a straight stitch with a medium stitch length.

STEP 4: ELASTIC MAGIC

Measure around your chest, right underneath your bust. Cut a piece of ⅛-inch-wide elastic to this measurement, plus 1 inch. Repeat these steps for your wrists. For example, if the circumference of your wrist is 6 inches, cut two lengths of elastic that each measure 7 inches in length.

Using the ruching technique you learned on p. 19, sew the elastic to the top, following the under-bust line you chalked. Do the same at the end of each sleeve.

STEP 5: IT'S PLEASANT TO PEASANT

Try on your new peasant top, proof that muu-muus can be cute!

Less Rock, More Rack!

The '80s may have produced some great music, but they also produced some pretty bad fashion (and hairstyles!). The good news is that means there's more for the pickin' when you go a-thriftin'. Look for the cheesiest Bon Jovi™ video-worthy dress you can find, the kind with the fitted bodice and a sweetheart neckline (shoulder pads and a pencil skirt are extra credit). We're going to take that dress and turn it into a figure-hugging corset. You want to find a dress with a bodice you like. Don't worry about the fit; in fact, it's a good thing if the bodice is a little too small. After you're done with this project, use the leftover material to make matching earrings (see The Vest Earrings in Town on p. 49)!

WHAT YOU'LL NEED
* '80s dress
* 2 yards of ribbon
* grommets (optional)

TECHNIQUES YOU'LL USE
* straight stitch
* cutting
* buttonholes

TIME TO COMPLETE
2 hours

STEP 1: CHALK MARKS THE SPOT

Begin by slipping the dress onto Ms. Trouble, inside out. If the dress doesn't fit around her chest, pin it so that it stays up. Use chalk to mark cut lines running from the top of the bust underneath the armpit, then to the back. You want the piece you ultimately cut out to re-semble a bustier. Chalk another line at the waist, where you are going to cut the skirt off.

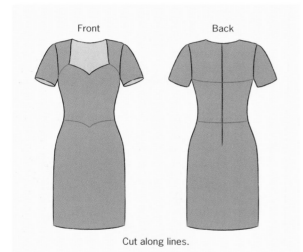

Front   Back

Cut along lines.

STEP 2: CUTS LIKE A KNIFE

Take the dress off Ms. Trouble and use a nice, sharp pair of scissors and cut along your chalk-lines. The dress probably has a zipper, so go ahead and cut that out, too.

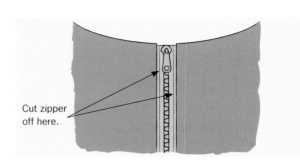

Cut zipper off here.

STEP 3: CHECK YOUR FRAY AT THE DOOR

You should now have what looks like a corset! Using a straight stitch with a medium stitch length, sew a line ½ inch in from the cut edges, all the way around. This will minimize any fraying around the cut edges. If you like a more finished look, you can also fold the cut edges over ½ inch and hem them.

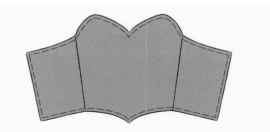

STEP 4: BUTTONHOLE LOVE

We're almost there, but you're going to need to keep that corset on somehow! We need to make a few buttonholes in the back of the corset that you can string ribbon through. Using a few

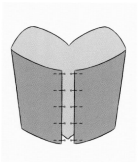

straight or safety pins, mark several spots 1½ inch to 2 inches apart on both sides of the opening of the corset.

Once you have the spots marked, set your sewing machine to make a buttonhole and sew buttonholes (see p. 27) where each of your pins are placed. You can also use grommets to reinforce the holes, or skip the buttonholes altogether and just use grommets.

STEP 5: TIE ONE ON

String the ribbon through the buttonholes and rock that corset!

EVERYTHING BUT THE KITCHEN SINK

- ☆ Checkbook Love: Game Point!
- ☆ Cuff 'Em!
- ☆ I Dream of Groceries
- ☆ Sock It to Me
- ☆ Hike That Skirt!
- ☆ Touchdown, Toiletries!
- ☆ Domestic Sun Goddess
- ☆ Vest-a-licious
- ☆ This Shirt Is the Sheet
- ☆ Boa-fy a Boudoir Basic

Now that you've mastered tops, pants, and dresses, it's time to broaden your horizons by exploring the rest of the store, which generally includes everything but the kitchen sink. Check out bedding, sporting goods, accessories, and whatever other sections you can find! Find cool buckles and snaps on purses, unusual materials in sporting goods, and yards and yards of usable fabrics disguised as duvet covers, sheets, and blankets. Even old bathrobes can be transformed into something really hot. Now get a move on and sink your teeth into your next thrifting adventure!

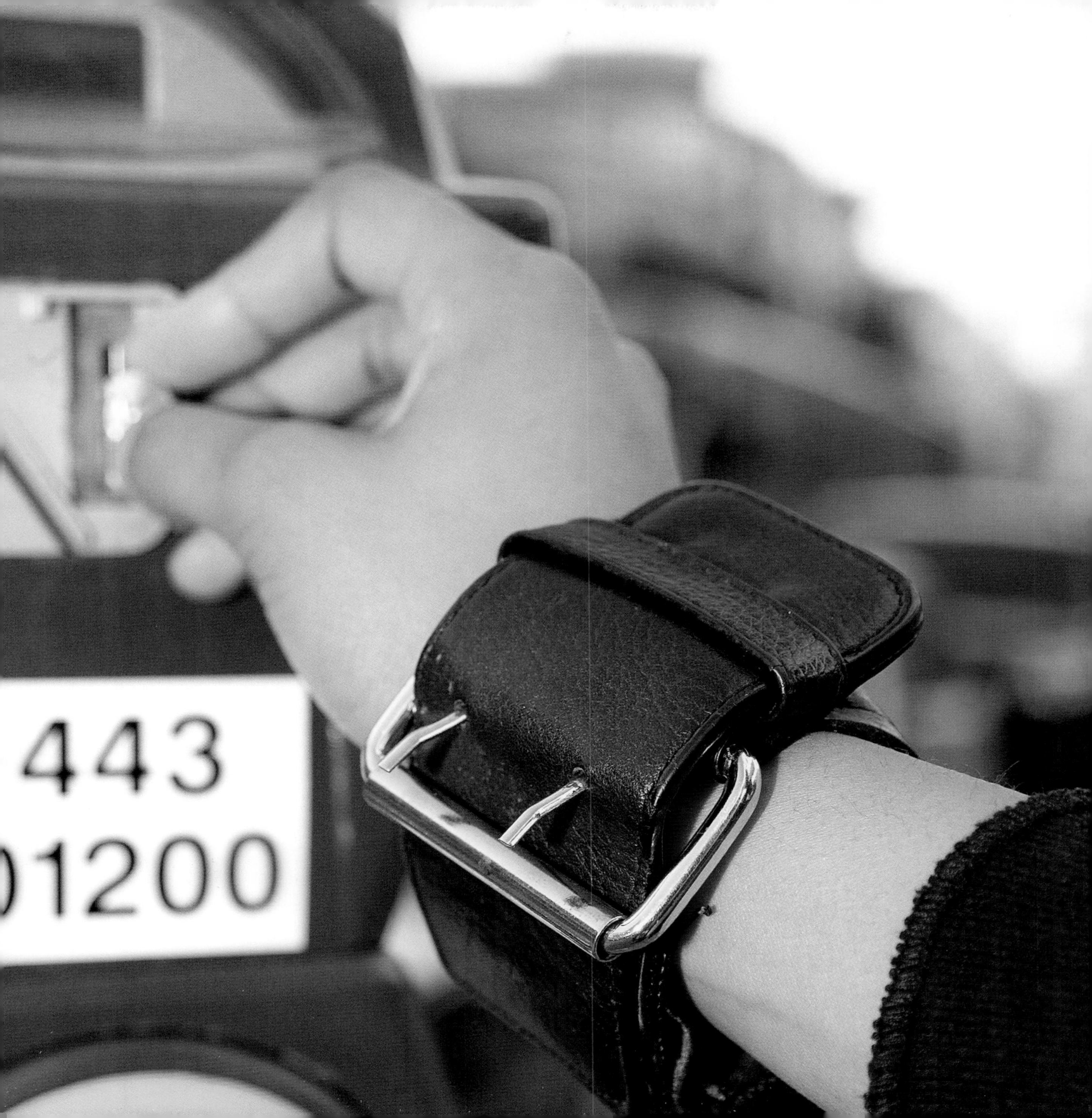
443
01200

Checkbook Love: Game Point!

Most people have sporting goods that will eventually get passed along to Goodwill, either because of equipment upgrades or because, well, they move on to a new hobby. Alissa Anderson from Mittenmaker shows us just how many treasures you can find in that section: She makes a great line of wallets from recycled tennis racket covers. Our project is inspired by her work, but instead of a wallet, we show you how to transform a tennis racket cover into a checkbook cozy. Hey, you may be paying off a parking ticket, but at least you'll look good doing it!

WHAT YOU'LL NEED
* tennis racket cover
* tissue paper
* leather or denim needle (optional)

TECHNIQUES YOU'LL USE
* straight stitch
* turning corners

TIME TO COMPLETE
1 hour

STEP 1: SERVING UP SOME CHECKBOOK LOVE

Get your chalk and draw an 8-inch by 7-inch rectangle on the front of your tennis racket cover. This will be the outside of your checkbook cozy, so be sure to place the logo or design accordingly. Cut along your chalked lines, cutting only the front cover.

STEP 2: IT'S A DOUBLES GAME

On the back of the tennis racket cover, chalk and cut two 3½-inch by 7-inch rectangles. You

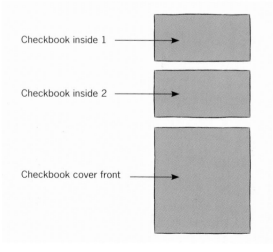

Checkbook inside 1

Checkbook inside 2

Checkbook cover front

should now have three rectangles cut out of the racket cover.

STEP 3: GRAND-SLAM VINYL SEWING

If your tennis racket cover is made of thick vinyl, you may need to replace the needle in your machine with a leather or denim needle. Some machines can handle thick vinyl with just a standard size 11 needle. If you're not sure, do a test swatch as described on the next page.

STEP 4: ACING THE GAME

Place the two 3½-inch by 7-inch rectangles

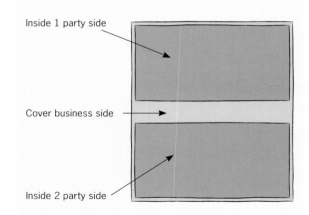

Inside 1 party side

Cover business side

Inside 2 party side

so they line up, business side to business side, with the top and bottom edges of the larger rectangle.

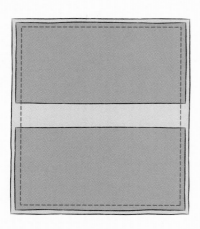

Using your newfound vinyl sewing skills, sew a ½-inch seam around the larger rectangle, turning corners along the way.

STEP 5: YOU'RE THE TOP SEED IN STYLE

Slip your checks inside their new cozy and serve up some serious fiduciary style!

Quick Set Break

To determine if you need to change to a leather or denim needle, do a test swatch using some of the leftover material from your tennis racket cover. Set your machine to sew a straight stitch with a long stitch length. Cut a small swatch of the vinyl, fold it in half, and sew a seam. If your machine punches through two layers of vinyl with its current needle, then you're good to go! If not, change your needle now—broken sewing machine needles aren't fun.

Sewing vinyl is tricky because your sewing machine's foot sticks to the vinyl's surface. Some people use a walking foot or Teflon foot when working with this material, but there's a simple solution: Tissue paper, the kind you stuff inside gift bags. Put the tissue paper between the foot and the vinyl when you're sewing, and the foot will glide along like *buttah*. When you're done sewing, just tear the tissue paper away, and *voilà*! You're looking at a perfect stitch, crafty lady!

Cuff 'Em

Thrift shops have tons of old purses with great closures. Look for a bag with interesting buckles or snap closures. We're going to turn that bag into a wrist cuff or bracelet and use the closure to latch the bracelet together.

WHAT YOU'LL NEED
* purse with cool closure
* leather or denim needle (optional)

TECHNIQUES YOU'LL USE
* straight stitch

TIME TO COMPLETE
1 hour

STEP 1: GET THE GIST OF YOUR WRIST
Start by measuring your wrist. You'll need this measurement to fit your wrist cuff.

STEP 2: CUT AROUND, CUT UP, AND GET DOWN
Open up your purse and lay it flat. Chalk and cut

a straight line on either side of the closure on the top flap of the bag from the closure to the edge, as illustrated below.

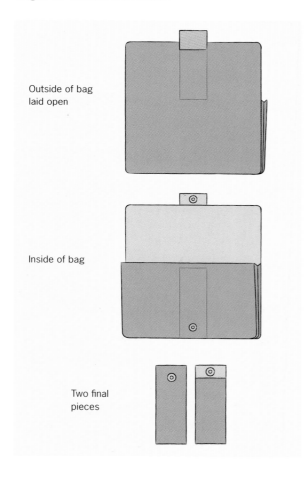

Outside of bag laid open

Inside of bag

Two final pieces

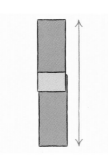

Do the same around the outside of the bag from the closure to the edge, as illustrated at left. You should have two pieces cut out of the purse, with one end that attaches to the other at the closure.

STEP 3: FIT IT BIT BY BIT

Figure out if the existing pieces will fit around your wrist. Close the two pieces together and measure from top to bottom edge.Eventually, you will sew these two pieces together, so remember to account for the seam allowance. In other words, if your wrist is 7 inches around, you will need a 7½-inch bracelet (assuming a ½-inch seam allowance and a snug-fitting wrist cuff). If the bracelet measurement works as is, great! If the measurement is too long, trim off the excess material from one side. If you need to add more length to the bracelet, simply cut a piece from the remaining material to sew on to one end. Remember to factor in the seam allowance!

STEP 4: PUT IT ALL TOGETHER

If your purse is made of leather, replace your current needle with a leather needle now. Layer the pieces you are sewing together so the business side of one piece faces the party side of the other.

If you need to add some length to your current pieces, you can do so now by sewing the extra material you cut to one side of the cuff, using a straight stitch with a long stitch length. If no extra material is needed, go ahead and sew the cuff pieces together.

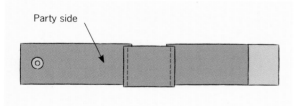

Party side

STEP 5: WRIST CUFFS TO MAKE WONDER WOMAN PROUD

You're done! Now you've got some wrist décor *and* enough material left over to make matching earrings! (See "The Vest Earrings in Town," p. 49.)

I Dream of Groceries

Grandma-style flannel nightgowns and robes abound in secondhand stores. Snatch one up and turn it into a washable, recycled grocery bag!

WHAT YOU'LL NEED
❋ flannel nightgown or robe

TECHNIQUES YOU'LL USE
❋ straight stitch

TIME TO COMPLETE
45 minutes

STEP 1: CHECK OUT THE SCENARIO

Take a look at your nightgown. Does it have any cool pockets? Neat straps? Amazing accents? Envision using all the best parts to maximize your grocery bag's cuteness potential. In our example, the nightgown included a belt with fun scalloped edges, so we're going to use it to make straps.

Decide on the size of your bag (you can use a standard plastic grocery bag as a good estimate for width). Add 1 inch to your desired width for seam allowance, and use chalk to mark the nightgown where you will cut. Generally, grandma nightgowns have the same pattern all over, so it doesn't really matter where you cut from; just make sure it will all fit. The easiest way to start is to match up with an edge.

STEP 2: GET STRAPPY

If you don't have a belt to use, you will also need to cut out straps. For these, use what's left of the nightgown, or get funky and use contrasting ribbon or random scrap fabric.

Decide how long you want your straps by draping a tape measure over your shoulder to where you would want the tote to sit. Add 1 inch for the seam allowance. We decided on 2½ feet (so it hangs down 1¼ feet from the shoulder) and allowed 1 inch for seam allowance.

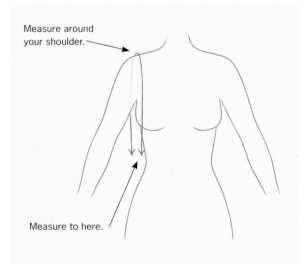

Measure around your shoulder.

Measure to here.

How wide do you want your straps to be? Since they will be load-bearing, we recommend straps that are at least 2 inches wide to distribute the weight. Take the number you decide on, double it, and add 1 inch for seam allowance. So, since we want the straps to be 2 inches wide, our strap pieces need to be cut 5 inches wide.

STEP 3: CUT AWAY!

Cut the bag and straps based on your desired measurements. The front and back pieces of the tote should be the same size, as should both of the straps.

STEP 4: GET SEWING

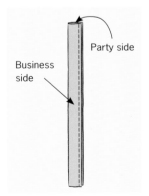

Party side

Business side

If you are making straps, fold your first strap piece in half like a long taco shell, with the party sides facing each other on the inside of the taco. Sew a seam, using a straight stitch with a medium stitch length and a ½-inch seam allowance, creating a long tube.

Turn the tube right-side out. To make your strap lay flat, sew a straight stitch ½ inch from the edges, down each long side. (Hint: Iron the strap flat after you turn it inside out, which makes the sewing a little easier.) Repeat to make the second strap.

STEP 5: GET BAGGY

Facing the party sides of your tote pieces to each other, sew down one of the side seams using a ½-inch seam allowance.

To hem the top edge of the bag, open the bag and fold down the top ½ inch of your bag so the cut edge is on what will be the inside of your finished tote. Pin it down and sew this edge down.

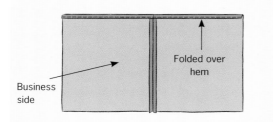

Business side

Folded over hem

Matching the top sides of the bag pieces together again, sew the other side seam with a ½-inch seam allowance. (See the illustration below left.)

STEP 6: GET STRAPPY, ONE MORE TIME

Pin the straps on the inside of the tote where you think they should go and try on your bag to be sure. Sew the straps down by stitching on top of the thread line you just made to hem the top edge of the tote.

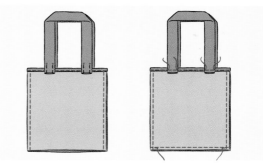

Finish off your tote by sewing together the bottom of the bag. With the bag business-side out, stitch the bottom closed using a ½-inch seam allowance. Make sure you backtack, as this is the part of the bag that carries the most stress.

Sock It to Me

Busy sewer that you are, you may not have time to run around picking up appropriate hostess gifts. (You have clothes to sew and thrift shops to hit up!) But, a subversive sewer never arrives at a party empty-handed! While you are out looking for the treasures that will be your next outfits, make sure to pick up some cute kneesocks or wool stockings to create the perfect wine cozy gift. Try to find a funky kneesock—just make sure your socks or stockings are big enough to hold a bottle of wine. If the store doesn't carry kneesocks to your liking, grab a men's shirt and tie and check your copy of *Sew Subversive: Down & Dirty DIY for the Fabulous Fashionista* for other wine bag ideas.

WHAT YOU'LL NEED
long, tube-shaped kneesock—clean, please!

TECHNIQUES YOU'LL USE
straight stitch

TIME TO COMPLETE
15 minutes

STEP 1: STRATEGIZE

Turn the sock inside out and insert the bottle of wine (or champagne or sparkling cider). Determine where you'd like the top of the sock to hit the bottle. We like it to land around the neck of the bottle so you can hold both the bag and the bottle securely in one hand while hailing a cab with the other.

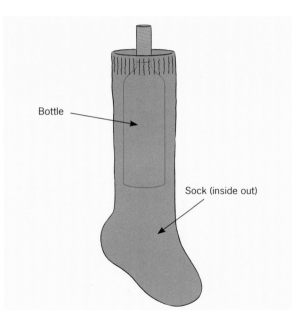

Bottle

Sock (inside out)

STEP 2: PIN

Laying the bottle and sock on their side, pin the sock closed right below the bottom of the bottle. (If there is a cute pattern on the front of the sock that you want to take advantage of, turn the sock right-side out and peek at the placement before cutting.)

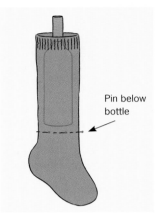

Pin below bottle

STEP 3: CUT AND SEW

Remove the bottle and cut the sock ½ inch below where you pinned. Sew along the pin line (either by hand or by machine), turn it party-side out, insert bottle, and head out to the festivities!

Hike That Skirt!

A mesh football jersey is your best bet for a great A-line skirt. The mesh makes for a fashionable companion to the vintage slip you'll also be using. Make sure the jersey you choose is wide enough through the torso to fit around your hips and tush (don't shop in the kids' section for this one). Find a vintage slip that looks good with the jersey's colors. You'll be using the length of the slip for the overall skirt, so make sure it is a length you like (we went with just below the knee).

WHAT YOU'LL NEED
* sports jersey
* silky slip

TECHNIQUES YOU'LL USE
* straight stitch
* ruching
* zigzag stitch

TIME TO COMPLETE
45 minutes

STEP 1: CUT 'EM OFF

Cut off the sleeves of your jersey, inside the seams, and cut a straight line along the top, just under the neckband. (Be sure to save the sleeves for another project!)

STEP 2: GO LONG

Cut the length of the jersey to be 2 to 3 inches shorter than the slip. This way, the slip will peek out from under the jersey. We cut along the top edge of our jersey, leaving the original bottom hem intact.

STEP 3: FORM FITTING

Using Ms. Trouble, fit the waist, hips, and width of the jersey loosely to your shape: Slide the jersey onto Ms. Trouble, business side out. Start at the waist, pin at either side, then pin along the side seams to match the form of your hips and the overall width of the skirt.

You won't want to size the jersey too tight; it will need to hang loosely over the slip. (The waist measurement of the jersey should be 2 to 4 inches larger than the actual measurement of your waist, or wherever you want the skirt waist to sit.) You can use the slip for reference by

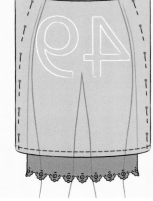

putting it on Ms. Trouble under the jersey (just be careful to not pin them together).

Remove the pinned jersey from Ms. Trouble and sew the seams you've pinned using a straight stitch with a short length. Cut out any excess jersey fabric along the seams.

STEP 4: THE MARRIAGE

Slide the jersey over the slip, with the business side of the jersey facing the party side of the slip (this is how it will look when you wear it) and fold over the top edge of the slip to cover the elastic. Pin down the fold in several places.

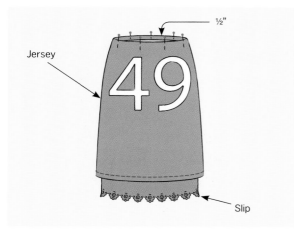

Sew down this folded edge using your ruching technique (see p. 19 for a brush-up), pulling the elastic band of the slip as you sew. Use a zigzag stitch with a medium length and width. We matched the thread color to the slip color to keep the waistband looking clean.

Sport this stylish skirt to the next *Monday Night Football* party, and you're sure to score a touchdown!

Touchdown, Toiletries!

Whether it's a professional sports team jersey or a little kid's soccer shirt, you're sure to find a colorful mesh treasure in any thrift store. You'll only the need the sleeve of the jersey (or both sleeves if you make a pair) to make this sporty toiletry bag. In the true fashion of recycling clothes, we used the sleeves left over from Hike That Skirt! (see p. 157). (We can't stand to waste a perfectly good mesh sports jersey sleeve!) You'll need a drawstring, too. Grab one from the waist of a pair of flannel pj's, or just use a string or cord that's about 2 feet long. We like the breathability of mesh, but if you can't find a mesh jersey, you can use any short-sleeved shirt to make this little toiletry bag.

WHAT YOU'LL NEED
* sports jersey
* drawstring or cord

TECHNIQUES YOU'LL USE
* casing
* straight stitch

TIME TO COMPLETE
30 minutes

STEP 1: IT'S HIP TO BE SQUARE

Cut the sleeve on the outside of the shoulder seam so you're left with a square or rectangle-shaped tube.

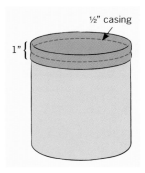

½" casing

1" {

STEP 2: CASING THE JOINT

Sew in a ½-inch casing along the edge, using a straight stitch with a medium stitch length (see p. 20 on sewing a casing).

STEP 3: CLOSING THE INNING

Turn the sleeve business-side out and pin the bottom edge together as shown in the drawing below; you're folding the edge without the casing. Sew one straight line, using a short stitch length, to close the bottom of your bag.

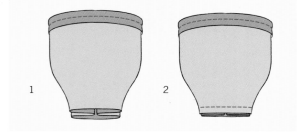

1   2

STEP 4: THE DRAWSTRING SHUFFLE

Using the tip of your scissors, a thread snip, or a seam ripper, make a small hole in the front edge of the casing (on the party side of the bag). This is the spot where you'll tie your drawstring, so make sure it looks good with the placement of the logo or number on the jersey. Tie a single knot at each end of the drawstring and pin a large safety pin to one end.

Feed the safety-pinned end of the drawstring into the hole and work it all the way around the casing until it comes back out. Remove the safety pin, fill up your toiletry bag with bathroom goodies, and tie that bad boy up. You're hotel-ready now!

> ### Tip
> • • •   • • •
>
> **Add some fabric scraps to the ends of the drawstrings for a fun detail!**

Domestic Sun Goddess

In the housewares section of your thrift store, you'll find a selection of aprons that are ripe to turn into apron dresses. Choose one with a bib-style top and a neck strap. We went with an old grocery-store uniform apron, but a homemade vintage apron would be just as cute and a little more girly. You'll also need some extra fabric that matches the apron. Since you're already in the housewares section, pick out a sheet or pillowcase. If the sheet you used for This Shirt Is the Sheet (see p. 175) looks good with your apron, you can use some of that leftover fabric, too.

WHAT YOU'LL NEED
* bib-style apron
* sheet

TECHNIQUES YOU'LL USE
* hemming
* straight stitch
* topstitching
* buttonhole-making (optional)

TIME TO COMPLETE
45 minutes

STEP 1: COVER YOUR REAR

Try on your apron. If the back panels overlap by at least 5 inches, you're one lucky lady, and you

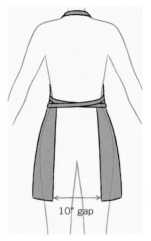

get to skip this step. If you're like us, and the apron doesn't cover your backside entirely, you'll be using the sheet fabric to fill in the gap.

Measure and cut two identical panels from the sheet to fill in the skirt of your

sundress. Measure the length of the apron's side edge and add 1 inch for hemming (allowing ½ inch at both the top and the bottom of each panel). Cut the panels to this length. We made the width of each panel equal to the gap between the apron edges (you can just estimate from when you tried it on), making sure to add an extra inch for seam allowance on one side, and hem allowance on the other.

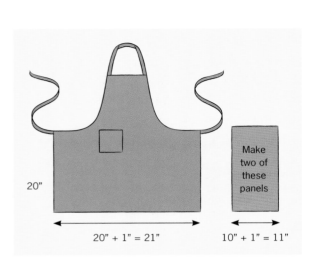

STEP 2: HEM THE EDGES

Iron down ½-inch folds on three sides of each panel. Make sure that you leave the side that will be sewn to the apron rough and hem the other edges using a medium-length straight stitch.

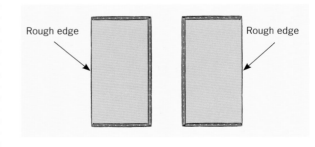

STEP 3: ATTACH THE BOOTY PANELS

Face the party side of the apron to the party side of the panels (along the rough edges) and pin each panel to the apron. Sew the panels to the apron.

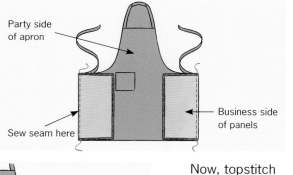

Party side of apron

Business side of panels

Sew seam here

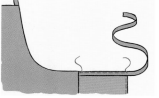

Now, topstitch the apron's waist ties to the top edge of the panels.

STEP 4: THE FINISHING TOUCHES

Using the buttonhole feature on your sewing machine, make a buttonhole on one side of the apron at the side of the waist (see p. 27 for buttonholes). Be sure to sew the buttonhole

large enough so your waist tie will fit though. If you don't want to make a buttonhole, you can

Buttonhole

just cut a small slit using scissors, thread snips, or a seam ripper. We made an official buttonhole to be sure that the waist slit won't unravel or tear.

Try on your sundress by wrapping one side over the other and pulling the waist tie through the small slit you just cut. Tie a bow or knot to keep it all together. If the neckband is too long or loose (Hint: If the Girls are hanging out on the sides, the neckband is too loose), take off the dress, go over to your sewing machine, and take in the neckband.

If you chose a plain apron and you want to spice it up a bit, try adding some decorative topstitching, sewing on a patch pocket, or pinning on a few fabric flowers. Plain or decorated, this backless sun goddess dress will earn you quite a few compliments at the next picnic, lake party, or afternoon shopping spree.

Vest-a-licious

Warm and cozy vests are amazing. Whether they're puffy or fleecy-soft, vests are a wonderfully practical component of any layering system. For this project, raid the bedding department of your local thrift shop and turn a bedspread, comforter, or fleece blanket into a stylish vest. You can also use a sleeping bag if you can find a rectangular one filled with a synthetic fill, rather than down. The same advice goes for the comforter; you don't want feathers to fly when you start to cut.

WHAT YOU'LL NEED
* comforter, bedspread, fleece blanket, or sleeping bag
* paper
* pen or pencil

TECHNIQUES YOU'LL USE
* straight stitch
* zigzag stitch

TIME TO COMPLETE
3 hours

STEP 1: PUT ON YOUR MATHEMAGICIAN HAT
We'll be making a pattern for this project, but before we get cutting, we need to take a few

measurements to make sure this pattern fits you. You can either take these measurements from your own body or Ms. Trouble's:

A = Length from top of neck to top of hip (you can measure to the top of your forehead for a large, luscious, fold-over collar)

B = Top of neck to end of shoulder

C = Circumference of shoulder

D = Bust circumference

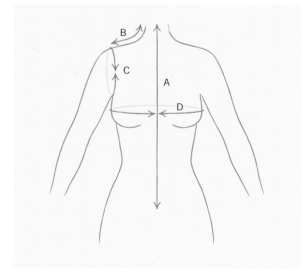

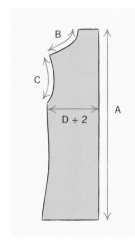

We'll be using these measurements to draw the pattern at left.

This pattern is very flexible, and mistakes don't show much, so don't worry about drawing the pattern perfectly, just try to get an approximation.

We'll use some simple math to tailor the pattern to you:

A = Length from top of neck to top of hip + 3 inches

B = Length from edge of shoulder to top of neck + 3 inches

C = (Circumference of shoulder + 3 inches) ÷ 2

D = (Bust circumference + 6 inches) ÷ 4

STEP 2: PITTER PATTERN

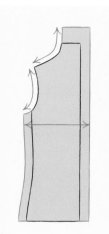

The measurements you took correspond to the pattern you make as shown at left.

Now, draw the pattern so that it reflects your measurements. Once you've got the pattern down, cut the pattern out so you can use it as a template.

STEP 3: SCISSOR SISTER

Lay the blanket out on your worktable or the floor. If you're working with a sleeping bag, cut out the zipper now.

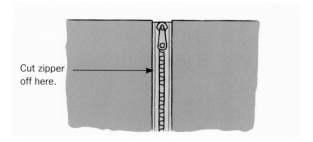

Cut zipper off here.

Lay the pattern up against the edge of the blanket so that the top right corner of the pattern lines up with the top right corner of the blanket.

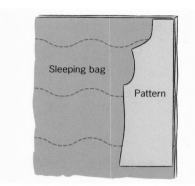

Sleeping bag

Pattern

Chalk a line onto the blanket, tracing around the pattern. Flip the pattern over and do the same on the other side.

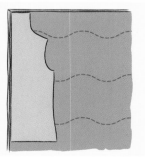

One everything is chalked, cut these pieces out. Now fold the remaining material in half and line the pattern up with your fold line. Chalk a line around the pattern again, using a sharp pair of scissors to cut through both layers of the folded blanket. If the blanket slides around while you're cutting, use a few straight or safety pins to pin through both layers to hold them in place while you're cutting.

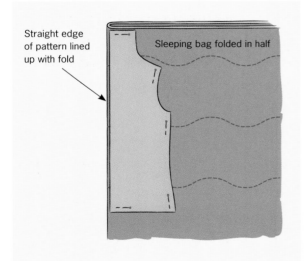

Straight edge of pattern lined up with fold

Sleeping bag folded in half

You should now have three pieces: two front pieces (1 and 2) and the back piece (3).

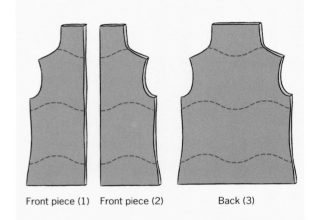

Front piece (1)   Front piece (2)   Back (3)

STEP 4: STITCH IT GOOD

After all that prep work, it's time for the fun part. Set your machine to a straight stitch with a medium to long stitch length. Take pieces 1 and 3 and line up the curved edges so that the party side of piece 1 faces the party side of piece 3. Sew two seams so that the pieces are attached at B (the neck seam), and at the side.

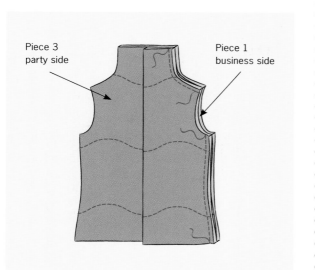

Repeat this step with pieces 2 and 3.

STEP 5: FINISH IT OFF

We're almost there! Now set your machine to make a zigzag stitch with a wide stitch width and a short to medium stitch length. On every unfinished edge (the armholes, the bottom hem, the front edges, and the neck), sew a zigzag stitch so that the zigzag wraps over the cut edge of the fabric, keeping it from unraveling.

Zigzag hangs over edge of fabric

This is kind of like lettuce edging (see p. 18), except you're not pulling the fabric before it goes underneath the presser foot. If you've used a fleece blanket, consider leaving the edges rough; they won't unravel, and it looks pretty cool.

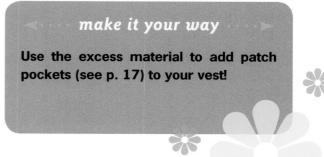

make it your way

Use the excess material to add patch pockets (see p. 17) to your vest!

This Shirt Is the Sheet

You may have never ventured into the linen section of your favorite thrift store, but you'd be surprised at how many sheets wind up there. Sheets are great to use as fabric because they're basically just big remnants of cloth. This batwing-style top uses a good deal of fabric, so a funky vintage sheet is just the thing. Pick any pattern that tickles your fancy, but choose a thinner sheet, as it will hang better on your body. If you can't find a sheet, you can also make this top out of a muumuu or a very large pillowcase. You'll also need a pair of suspenders that look good with your sheet. You'll just be using the elastic portion, so don't worry if the clasps are broken.

WHAT YOU'LL NEED
* sheet
* suspenders

TECHNIQUES YOU'LL USE
* straight stitch
* zigzag stitch
* hemming
* turning corners
* ruching

TIME TO COMPLETE
1 hour

STEP 1: THE DRAWING BOARD

Although this shirt is certainly not form-fitting, you still need a couple of measurements to get the pattern right for your body. Measure your torso length, arm span, waist, and neck. Add 4 inches to 6 inches to the wrist measurement (it will become a cute gather when the suspenders are added) and at the very least add 8 inches to 10 inches to your waist measurement. Feel free to add more if you want it to be more gathered.

The arm span measurement will depend on how long you want your sleeves. For a fuller shirt, we suggest that you add a couple of inches to each measurement.

The neck measurement should be wide enough so that your head can fit through the slit. We suggest using the distance between the tips of your collarbone; however, you may want to add an extra inch or so, depending on your own style.

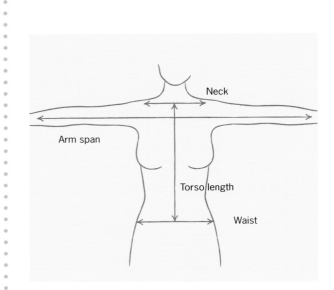

If you use a muumuu or anything other than a sheet for this project, start by cutting up the garment to create one piece of fabric that is big enough to fit this pattern—doubled, of course. Fold your sheet in half lengthwise (the fold will eventually be your shoulder line) and pin the sides together so they won't slip while you cut. Use the illustration as a guide, but alter the measurements to fit your body. Draw the pattern on your sheet using chalk or a pen.

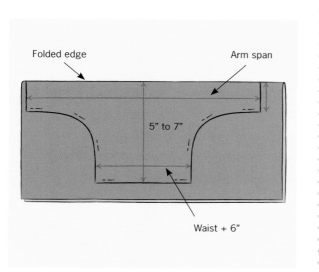

Folded edge

Arm span

5" to 7"

Waist + 6"

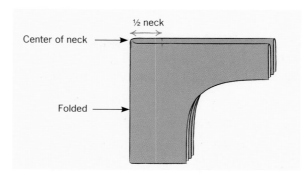

½ neck

Center of neck

Folded

STEP 2: THE CUTTING BOARD

With the two sides of the sheet pinned together, cut out the pattern you just drew. Remember to leave the folded edge intact! Once it's cut out, fold the fabric in half to find the center of the neck, and measure out on either side of center to mark the neck. Use some chalk or a pen to mark the neck measurement on the folded edge.

STEP 3: THE SEWING BOARD

If you still have any pins in your cut fabric, re-move them and locate the markings for the neck. Cut a slit between the markings. At each end of the slit, make a cut perpendicular to the slit extending ½ inch in each direction—you'll have a 1-inch cut on either side.

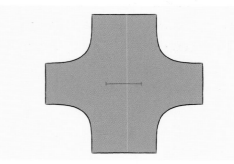

Take your cut piece over to the ironing board and iron down ½-inch folds along the neckline, with the party side turned in. Back at the sewing machine, sew down these folds. We used a medium-size zigzag stitch to add a little decoration, but a straight stitch with a medium length will do just fine. Sew around the entire neck hole, pivoting around the needle at the corners.

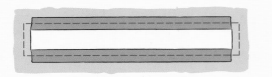

When the neck hole is done, fold the piece in half at the shoulder line, facing the party sides together, and sew along the batwings, making sure to keep the waist and armholes open. Use a straight stitch with medium stitch length and a ½-inch seam allowance.

STEP 4: THE RUCHING BOARD

You'll use the elastic from your suspenders for the waist and armbands of your top. Remove all the hardware from your suspenders and cut three pieces, one for the waistband and one for each armband. The lengths of your pieces will depend on your body and how tight you want the bands.

It doesn't matter which band you ruche first, but it is officially ruching time! (See p. 19 for a ruching refresher.) We started with the armbands—they're a little harder because of their small size. Remember to use the free arm of your machine for sewing tight spaces like this.

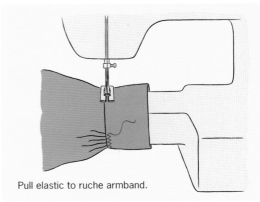

Pull elastic to ruche armband.

Finish off the waistband and do some spins with your arms out to the side, flaunting your suave style.

Boa-fy a Boudoir Basic

Sexy may not be the first word that comes to mind when you think of a fleece bathrobe. That's where subversive sewing comes in! You don't even need a sewing machine for this project. Pick up a bathrobe at your neighborhood secondhand store, grab your favorite fabric scissors, and get ready to transform that frump into fashion! You can use any large bathrobe for this project (one with a waist belt is a plus). We chose a fleece number, but if a flannel robe steals your heart, go for it! Our only caution is to avoid terry cloth. It becomes a mess when you cut into it, and it might get a little bulky around your neck.

WHAT YOU'LL NEED
* bathrobe
* scissors

TECHNIQUES YOU'LL USE
* cutting

TIME TO COMPLETE
2 hours

STEP 1: WAIST NOT, WANT NOT

Start by removing the waist belt from your robe and laying the robe out nice and flat. We're going to use the waist tie as the base for our fabulous boa! If your robe does not have a belt, cut a strip of fabric from the length of the robe. Make the strip about 1½ inches wide and 4 feet to 5 feet long.

STEP 2: STRIP IT GOOD!

Cut a bunch of 1-inch-wide by 8-inch-long strips of fabric from your fleece robe. We cut about 75 strips from our robe, but the exact number depends on the length of your waist belt. Estimate that you'll need about 1½ strips for every inch of waist belt you want to cover.

STEP 3: TIE ME UP, TIE ME DOWN

Starting on one end of the waist belt, tie the strips to the tie.

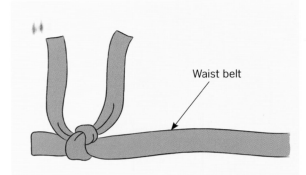

Waist belt

Continue until the entire length of the waist belt is covered in tied strips.

STEP 4: WHOA—A BOA!

Throw that boa around your neck and head to a party! You can stay out late—after all, you're partying in a bathrobe!

Resources

Garment Districts (for fabric and other fun stuff!)

Los Angeles
www.fashiondistrict.org

New York
www.fashioncenter.com

Secondhand Stores

Goodwill Industries International
www.goodwill.org

Buffalo Exchange
www.buffaloexchange.com

Crossroads Trading Co.®
www.crossroadstrading.com

Salvation Army
www.salvationarmyusa.org

Wasteland (Los Angeles and San Francisco)
www.thewasteland.com

Flipnotics Clothespad (Austin)
www.flipnotics.com

New Blanks to Play With

www.americanapparel.net

Clothing Swaps and Exchanges

Swap-O-Rama-Rama
www.swaporamarama.org

Garment Remake Exchange
www.garmentremake.com

The Clothing Swap
www.clothingswap.org

A Selection of Designers Who Refashion Vintage for Their Collections

Imitation of Christ by Tara Subkoff
Mittenmaker
www.mittenmaker.com

Armour Sans Anguish
www.armoursansanguish.com

Anti-Factory
www.anti-factory.com

Sewing Machine Manufacturers

Bernina®
www.berninausa.com

Singer®
www.singerco.com

Elna®
www.elna.com

Viking®
www.husqvarnaviking.com

Janome®
www.janome.com

Necchi®
www.necchi.it

Brother®
www.brother-usa.com

Baby Lock®
www.babylock.com

White®
www.whitesewing.com

Pfaff®
www.pfaff.com

Kenmore®
www.sears.com/kenmore

Notions Suppliers

Prym-Dritz (Stitch Witchery®, Fray Check™, sewing accoutrements)

Gütterman Thread

Other Places We Buy Machines

www.craigslist.org
www.ebay.com
Estate & yard sales

Crafty and Inspirational DIY Websites

www.craftster.org

www.getcrafty.com

www.garmentremake.com

www.sfcraftmafia.com

www.churchofcraft.org

supernaturale.com

www.instructables.com

www.notmartha.org

www.diynetwork.com

Other Websites We Like

www.styleindustry.com (resources for fashion industry)

www.patternreview.com (reviews on different brands and makes of sewing machines)

On-Line Sewing Supplies

Sew True
www.Sewtrue.com

Solo Slide
www.soloslide.com

Repro Depot Fabrics
(Great vintage reproduction and
retro themed fabrics)
www.reprodepotfabrics.com

National In-Store Sewing Supplies

Jo-Ann Fabrics
www.joann.com

Michaels
www.michaels.com

Hancock Fabrics
www.hancockfabrics.com

Magazines

Readymade
www.readymademag.com

Bust
www.bust.com

Craft
www.craftzine.com

Sew Stylish
www.sewstylish.com

Sewing Lounges

Stitch Lounge, Inc. (San Francisco)
www.stitchlounge.com

Stitches (Seattle)
www.stitchesseattle.com

Make Workshop (New York)
www.makeworkshop.com

First Samples (Austin)
www.firstsamples.com

The Sewing Lounge (MN)
www.sewinglounge.com

Textile Center (MN)
www.textilecentermn.org

SF Bay Area Fabric Stores

Discount Fabrics
 525 4th Street, San Francisco
 (415) 495-4201

 2315 Irving Street, San Francisco
 (415) 564-7333

 1432 Haight Street, San Francisco
 (415) 621-5584

 3006 San Pablo Avenue, Berkeley
 (510) 548-2981

Fabric Outlet
2109 Mission Street, San Francisco
(415) 552-4525

Mendel's Far Out Fabrics & Art Supplies
1556 Haight Street, San Francisco
(415) 621-1287

Darlene's Fabrics
2877 Mission Street, San Francisco
(415) 550-0149

Britex Fabrics
146 Geary Street, San Francisco
(415) 392-2910

Stone Mountain & Daughter Fine Fabrics
2518 Shattuck Avenue, Berkeley
(510) 845-6106

Poppy Fabric
5151 Broadway, Oakland
(510) 655-5151

Jo-Ann Fabrics & Crafts
75 Colma Boulevard, Colma
(650) 755-1711

Craft Fairs

Renegade Craft Fair (Brooklyn
and Chicago)
www.renegadecraft.com

Bazaar Bizarre (Boston, Los Angeles,
Cleveland, and San Francisco)
www.bazaarbizarre.org

Art vs. Craft (Milwaukee)
www.artvscraft.com

Crafty Wonderland (Portland)
www.craftywonderland.com

Ferria Urbana (San Francisco)
www.feriaurbanasf.com

Stitch Fashion Show and Guerrilla Craft
Bazaar (Austin)
www.stitchaustin.com

San Francisco Craft Mafia presents: Mafia
Made (San Francisco)
www.sfcraftmafia.com

Index

Note: **Bold** page numbers indicate that illustrations or photographs appear. (When only one number of a page range is **bold**, illustrations or photographs appear on one or more of the pages.)